The Power Of The Soul Over The Body, Considered In Relation To Health And Morals

George Moore

THE POWER

OF

THE SOUL OVER THE BODY.

THE

POWER OF THE SOUL

OVER THE BODY,

CONSIDERED

IN RELATION TO HEALTH AND MORALS.

BY

GEORGE MOORE, M.D.,

MEMBER OF THE ROYAL COLLEGE OF PHYSICIANS, LONDON,
ETC. ETC.

" Thou hast a noble guest, O flesh !"
St. Bernard.

LONDON:

LONGMAN, BROWN, GREEN, AND LONGMANS,
PATERNOSTER ROW.

——

MDCCCXLV.

CONTENTS.

PART I.

PART II.

PREFACE.

THIS sketch of the influence of the mind on the body, was commenced and continued with the feeling that the soul is the true object of affection, and that all its interests are essentially religious. The principal part of the volume was written several years since, during the unwelcome, but valuable, leisure of disease; for the purpose of being addressed to a few young men, who appeared to be deeply impressed with the nature and importance of the subject. On a re-perusal of the manuscript, the recollection of this encouragement induced a hope that the publication might find an apology in the approval of reflecting readers; especially as, at this time, the public mind is unusually roused to the observation of mental influences, in the production of remarkable phenomena under mesmerism and disease. The views exhibited in these pages, having been consolatory and instructive to himself, the author trusts will be deemed at least a good reason for his endeavour thus to obtain the attention of others. A corresponding volume, concerning Bodily Temperament, Will and Habit, was intended to have accompanied this, but it may more suitably follow, should public favour in any degree encourage the present adventure.

As said good old "*Ihon Caius, Docteur in Phisicke,*" A. D. 1552, "*man beying borne not for his owne vse and cōmoditie alone, but also for the commō benefite of many, (as reason wil and al good authores write) he whiche in this world is worthy to lyue, ought al ways to haue his hole minde and intente geuen to profite others. Which thynge to shewe in effecte in my self, although by fortune some waies I haue been letted, yet by that whiche fortune cannot debarre, some waies again I haue declared.*"

Hastings,
March 11th, 1845.

INTRODUCTION.

THE term soul has been preferred to stand in the
title of this volume, because in common discourse
it is employed to signify an individual intelligent
being, which actuates the body and is popularly
supposed to be capable of an active existence independent on physical connection. It is meant
to designate that which is conscious of acting,
thinking, and willing. To avoid confusion, the
words soul, mind, and spirit will be employed as
synonymous; because to distinguish their proper
shades of meaning would require a metaphysical
nicety incompatible with the purpose of this work.
We perceive the diversified operations of the thinking principle, and call it by different names according to its different manifestations; but the unity
of its nature, like that of God himself, is an announced or a revealed truth, to be received by
faith, because our faculties will not allow us yet
to comprehend an existence without parts. In

B

using the senses, we speak of the soul under the
term Sense; when inferring truth from truth, we
call it Understanding; when fancying the future,
Imagination; when reviewing the past, Memory;
when choosing or refusing, Will. Yet all our
faculties are but properties of one being, and we
feel our identity amidst all the diversity of our
thoughts and purposes.

We cannot explain the mode any more than the
nature of that which thinks; and mere endeavours
to define what we cannot demonstrate, neither
improve our faculties, nor advance our knowledge.
An elaborate disquisition on mind and matter,
would therefore be a useless demand on patience;
and since we cannot discover any thing concerning either but in their operations on each other,
if we would learn their relative importance, we
must study their reciprocal influence.

Some philosophers, perhaps forgetful that mind
is manifested by its own consciousness, have asserted that intelligence is but a result of material
constitution, and therefore that the decay or destruction of the physical organization, with which
it is at present connected, necessarily involves
also the everlasting dissolution of the thinking
principle. Whether true or false, this must be
a miserable conclusion; for it implies that our
Creator, if there be one, has formed his sentient
and intelligent creature—man, for no other pur-

pose than to witness for a short time his own paradoxical existence, to contrast his desires with his destiny, to shrink away in terror from the sight and the thought of all that is glorious, great, good, or enduring, and to shun all notion of Deity, lest what is thus presented to his apprehension, should excite aspiring wishes and build up lofty hopes, only that their destruction may be the more certain and the more extensive. The wondrous speculum, which restless research inspires man with ingenuity to fabricate, reflects the dim glimmerings of infinite worlds, into which he would direct his enquiring ken, only to kindle and expand and then becloud his reason; for to follow its promptings were merely madness, and wisdom would be impossible; even to know would be vanity and folly, unless we knew that existence might be equal to our felt capacity of enjoying it. Were a man sure that he could not possibly possess a better than this earthly life, to look off from this dull cold spot would only be to aggravate his doom. The glory of distant worlds would fall like a blight upon his being, for it will suggest possibilities of intelligence and delight for ever beyond his reach.

A creeping thing prepares for its perfection, and at length bursts from its silken tomb with newly-developed form, appetites and nature. Like a "winged flower," with brilliant and delicate

pinions and rich in gems, it gladly flutters with
the light, and sips nectar from the hand of God.

The grub may tend to be a butterfly, but why
should the worm just peeping from its clod aspire
to anything beyond the clay on which it is destined to crawl and rot? And why should man
look higher? Why? His spirit will not crawl, it
travels along with the light into infinite space,
and calculates on a life and a capacity commensurate with its desires. He is impelled by a
belief, which seems essential to his rational existence, that this beautiful world is not altogether a
delusive show; for he cannot think that the wondrous facts of creation teach him to look for the
end of truth only in death; but he feels that, in
proportion as his intellect expands and expatiates
in knowledge, does it aspire to immortality, and
when most intimate with the realities of time, his
reason finds stability, satisfaction, and rest, only
in communion with the Eternal.

All who have looked below the surface of
things, must account that science despicable, and
that philosophy pitifully meagre, which afford no
higher object of pursuit than a little sensuality;
no brighter prospect than a phantom life, no better
end than an endless death.

If believers in the material system of faith (it
demands great faith, such as it is,) indeed allow
that there is existence beyond things, if they do

allow a God, it certainly must be a god of their own. He cannot have revealed himself to the world, for there is not any reasonable pretence to a revelation but in the Bible; and therefore those who believe, in contradiction to that Book, the doctrine which teaches that the soul dies with the body, must have substituted their own opinions for the declarations of that venerable authority, and instead of worshipping Jehovah, or in any measure obeying his laws, they must have constituted themselves their own deity, and made their own glory and convenience the end of all their thoughts, and all their actions. Unhappy men! like fallen spirits their pride separates them both from divine and human sympathy,—they cannot believe that omnipotence is love, and therefore they cannot adore.

But there are those who tell us they have tasted a better philosophy, and they teach us to regard it as "a perpetual feast of nectared sweets," of which the more we partake, the more we enjoy, and indeed the effect of its fullest enjoyment is nothing short of actual participation in Divine nature. This philosophy regards man as formed to be instructed by acquaintance with good and evil in this world, that the will may be disciplined under moral and physical law, and having knowledge imparted, and motives presented to the soul, it may be the better qualified for introduction to an enlarged existence.

It is true, that in this state all intelligence that is not instinctive or intuitive is received only through the body, but yet our reason possesses perceptions of truth which sensation could never have conveyed, and all our reflections concerning our nature terminate in the conclusion which revelation warrants,—that the soul dies not. Even the lower creatures, down to creeping things, are endowed with knowledge, which they acquire not by the use of their senses. No sooner do they burst from their "procreant cradle" than instinct with skill they seek their happiness in the right path, as if directly illuminated by divine guidance. Why then should man be without this guidance in his instinctive endeavours after his proper enjoyment and in the possession of permanent blessedness? There is a light which, in the hope, lightens every man that cometh into the world.

In pursuing our theme it behoves us, who profess to be Christians, not to disregard the source from whence we derive our religion, but as far as we can, to conduct our inquiries as if we really felt the force of those truths which we profess to believe. Believers in revelation are not only preserved from the misery of the sceptic, but excited to larger inquiries than he. The man of faith must be a thinking man, for he infers from facts, and is directed as well as encouraged in his researches after every kind of truth; since the book that secures his faith, often supplies the subject and also indicates the proper direction of rational study. Here we learn our origin and our end; but without it mankind would have continued unable to discover either why, or whence they had their being. The Bible indeed finds the same faults with this world that common sense does,—sin, pain and death are in it; but then in the Bible only do we discover a promise of a perfect remedy for evil, in the re-adjustment of moral and material elements by God in man.

The sublimest and most interesting thoughts expressed in language, are contained in the Genesis given by Moses. In this we find that the production of man was the finishing stroke to creation—the Creator's especial thought, the final end of the six days' work. This earth appears to have been furnished for him by the creative word which said, "let light be," and light was. Man was then brought into being to behold *His* glory who formed our nature expressly in correspondence with Deity: "in the image of God created he him*. And as the dust was fashioned by the

---

* We have divine authority for understanding this expression to denote the moral excellence and dominion with which man was endowed.—Eph. iv. 24 : Col. iii. 10.

immediate touch of Jehovah's finger, the human structure took the impress of Divinity. That this form of earthly mould and heavenly meaning might not remain like the temple without its indwelling glory, God breathed within man's body the abiding spirit of various lives, and thus also illumined him with the moral reflection of the divine character. The Lord God formed man of the dust of the ground, and breathed into his nostrils the breath of life; and *"man became a living soul."* In these words we have a distinct announcement that life and mind did not manifest themselves as the organization of its structure proceeded, but that vitality and intelligence were superadded, in connection with a separate existence directly imparted from Jehovah, and therefore in immediate relation with Him.

Thus man walked forth in his paradise at once the representative and the worshipper of Love, and Light, and Power, connecting the visible with the invisible worlds in his own person, and by the union of spirit with matter, feebleness with perfection, exhibiting the glorious mystery of creation,—Omnipotence revealed in contradictions reconciled. Man is the grand contradiction —a compound of paradoxes; for he is constituted not only of opposites, but of contraries. In studying ourselves, therefore, we become intimate with the greatest difficulties and the greatest interests.

As before observed, the co-existence of mind with matter in one being is quite beyond our comprehension but not beyond our knowledge, for we experience the fact. The reason of our compound constitution is, simply, that the Great Spirit has willed our adaptation to a physical world, from whence we are to derive intelligence and enjoyment. We find, however, that our minds are governed by laws that have nothing to do with material organization; for our sense of right and wrong, truth and falsehood, virtue and vice, has no relation to bodily structure, but as the vehicle and instrument of mind. We conceive ideas, combine, reason, not according to atomic affinities, but to spiritual associations. We love, hope, fear, if not irrespective of external impressions, at least without their continuance. Above all, we retain amidst the changes of our bodies and the shifting variety of decay around us, a distinct consciousness of our own identity, and an intuitive conviction, as far as reason is awakened, that we hold our faculties and endowments, not from the fortuitous action of nature, as a blind power, but from the purpose of God as an informing spirit, in whom we live, and move, and have our being for ever.

Whatever will tend to confirm our confidence in this position will add to our happiness, and it is hoped that the examination of facts which illustrate our nature, will constrain us as with the force of a rational necessity, practically to acknowledge our dependance, while it encourages our reliance, on Him who remembers we are dust and breathes on us his spirit. The highest thought is of eternal Being. All real adoration is the feeling of a life beyond sense, and which organization cannot contain nor manifest, much less produce. It is the proceeding spirit acknowledging in love the parent spirit; it is the communion of the Father and the Son; an entrance into the glory which was before the world. From everlasting to everlasting, thou art, O Infinite! The human mind would sink crushed by the burden of the vast thought if thou didst not in humanity sustain thy creature. Enable us, O God, to reflect upon thine image in reverence, and to honor thy majesty as revealed in the fearfully wondrous frame and in the moral excellence of man.

Every sentient creature is characterized by its dispositions. The provision made for its enjoyment, and also the peculiarities of its physical endowment, must be in keeping with its will. If, then, we would ascertain the true dignity and destiny of man, we must study the scope and power of that principle in him, and how it is influenced; for in fact the mind or soul is thus especially manifested in the body. We may conveniently regard the power of the soul in the following respects :—

1st. As manifested in the senses, in attention, and in memory.

2ndly. In the influence of mental determination and emotion over the vital functions of the body.

THE

POWER OF THE SOUL OVER THE BODY.

~~~~~~~~~~~~~~~~~

PART I.

THE SOUL, AS MANIFESTED IN THE USE OF THE SENSES, IN ATTENTION AND IN MEMORY.

THE POWER

OF

THE SOUL OVER THE BODY.

CHAPTER I.

THE ADAPTATION OF THE BODY TO THE SOUL.

THROUGHOUT that part of creation within our scope, we behold evidences of infinite wisdom; and whenever effects are traced to causes, and formation is considered in respect to its design, we discover a perfect adaptation of means to ends, —the apparatus being exactly suited to its purpose, without defect, without redundancy.

When surveying any living creature, we naturally inquire, why it is provided with such and such peculiarities of organization. In answer to the inquiry we learn that every peculiarity of formation is adapted to some instinct of the creature, or accommodates it the better to the circumstances in which the Creator has placed it. Monstrosities rarely happen, and only confirm the rule, for they too occur according to certain laws, which prove still more clearly than could be proved without them, to our intellect at least, that the will, which designs, and the power which executes, calculated on the disorder that created will produces, and set bounds to its interference which cannot be passed.

We cannot with propriety say that one complete animal is nobler than another, because of any prominence of particular organs as compared with its whole body; nor is one creature to be called monstrous or ugly, in comparison with another, for each is exactly fitted to its place in the grand scale of existence, and therefore all are alike beautiful, as exhibiting the wonderful wisdom and beneficence of God. But creation is graduated, and every creature has its proper place. The totality of an animal's framework indicates its position on the scale of being. If we measure man according to this standard, his superiority is at once evident. Not that his body is distinguished by any marked excellence in those qualities which empower brutes, but by the symmetrical accordance of all its parts for superior purposes, under the direction of a will that cannot truly sympathize with lower natures.

" Os homini sublime dedit, cœlumque tueri,
Jussit et erectos ad sidera tollere vultus."

This is a fine heathen sentiment, but not quite true; for the eye of man was intended to search

the earth as well as the heavens, and to behold
Omnipotence in every part of the universal temple. The face is indeed the index of thought and
sentiment, the medium through which mind most
vividly communicates with mind, but yet the
whole body acts together in the full expression of
feeling :—

" Totamque infusa per artus,
Mens agitat molem."

Let us imagine a human figure as if now standing before us, like the Apollo of the intellectual
Greeks when he gazed on the smitten Python.
We seem to see in this statue the visible idea or
image of the man who aspired to be a god. At
length he stands triumphant over the temptation
and the tempter; content in the consciousness of
a renovated and perfect humanity. Passion and
intellect are blended in calm unison; knowledge
and affection are at peace; the attributes of feeling, thought and action, are combined in one attitude, expressive of the delicate might of a living
spirit. The mind reigns in that body. The in-
carnate intelligence manifestly controls matter by
his will, and appears as if conscious of being always resisted, yet never vanquished; but, inspired
by the apprehension of his right, as vicegerent
of Almightiness, he subdues resistance and sur-
mounts difficulties by perseverance in the use of
strength, that continually and spontaneously in-

creases with every opposition to his purpose. Such
is man, when sustained by the divinity which stirs
within him; the only creature on which the Creator has shadowed divine perfections, and therefore
he is to be honored even in his ruin, for when his
affections, and faculties are restored, as they may
be, to divine sympathy, he shall again stand up-
right, the conqueror of the mighty serpent.

We have looked upon man in his highest aspect,

> " God-like, erect, with native honour clad,
> In naked majesty."

But even if we regard him in his most uncultivated condition, where the intellect is left to the
freedom of the elements, and educated only by
the forces of corporeal necessity, we yet shall see
much indication of his dignity.

The wild barbarian awakes to action, and every
movement speaks of thought.   He is evidently
influenced by a world within him, where reflection and anticipation present incessant business
for his spirit, and he will not live in the solitude
of his own perceptions, but he seeks the higher
pleasures of sociality and fellowship.   His ideal
existence is as actual as that of his body and
crowded with emotions.   Memory and imagination people a world of their own, in the busy
scenes of which he dwells more thoroughly and
intimately than in that which is present to his
outward senses.   And he reveals his inner life by

living language. He talks of what he feels, not
only in words but also in the lineaments of his
face, and while he speaks he stretches out his
hand towards some object which may illustrate
his words, or interest his companion, and thus by
the very act of pointing, at once declares himself
superior in endowment to every earthly creature,
except his fellow-man; for no other holds rational
discourse, or even possesses that simple adjunct
to human intelligence, the power of distinctly
and designedly pointing, to direct the attention of
another.

We say then that the existence of a resident
and superintending mind, a thinking principle,
an intelligent spirit operating upon the body, in
it, not of it, might be inferred from the external
form alone; and the manner of every movement
and expression of that form, proves how perfectly
it was adapted for the use of a guiding and dominant spirit, pervading, informing, and employing it.

As the habits of certain animals have been correctly inferred from the examination of detached
portions of their structure, so from almost any
part of man's body we may at once discover that
it was constructed for the accommodation and
delight of an intellectual being. Even those dis-
advantages, in regard to the coarser physical
qualities which lower animals possess, act but as

stimuli to the human faculties, which supply all
deficiencies, and confer the best accommodation.
In fact, the excellence of man consists in the
delicate adaptation of his structure, for without
this the reasoning principle would be out of place.
He is the most delicate creature on the earth, but
yet he is not formed to hide himself. He must
indeed be intrusted at first to the tenderest care
of affection, to be nurtured into strength enough
to endure the action of the elements amidst which
he is destined to dwell, yet he alone comes forth
from his feeble infancy, erect, the observed, and
the observer, with a *mind* to plan, and a *hand* to
execute. The instrument is adapted to the agent
—"*Non enim manus ipsæ homines artes docuerunt,
sed ratio.*"* But if man's body had been constituted on any inferior model, art and science could
have had no outward existence, and reason must
have been imprisoned, in brute form. Supposing
human knowledge then possible, man could only
have been manifest as a subtle beast. "It is
mind that makes the body rich," but the soul
needs a corresponding body, and God has wedded
them together, in perfect suitability to their present business and abode.

How inconceivably exact must be the adaptation of the body to the purposes of the mind!
The organs of sense and of action so instanta-

* Galen.

neously and perfectly obey the demands of the will that in many of our most complicated and ordinary movements we are unconscious of having willed to employ the body, but it seems to have consented to anticipated intention in such a manner that we feel identified with it. So complete is the accordancy and assent between a healthy body and a sensual mind that some persons scarcely acquire a thought that takes them out of the body, they live only in its sensations. The machine which they actuate is confounded with themselves, because it so admirably obeys their wills that they conceive no other enjoyment, and reach not so far as an idea of moral or spiritual excellence when habituated to the pleasures of sense.

While the system is in the highest state of health, that is, when best adapted for use, so great is the enjoyment of this perfect fitness that we can scarcely avoid putting our limbs into action, or as we say exerting ourselves, hence dancing becomes the natural expression of healthy gladness, for on these vigorous occasions we cannot meditate, but our life and thought are altogether bent on muscular activity, or the use of the body irrespective of reflection. This happy activity is beautifully exemplified in healthy children, whose business appears to be merely to enjoy action and unmeaning pastime, and to exercise the senses simply for the pleasure thus afforded.

But how exquisitely the spirit becomes visible
in every attitude and every feature of happy children! We read their thoughts and feelings as
perfectly as if their souls were our own. And
were our minds and bodies attuned by love, we
should find ourselves impelled by sympathy to
join their sport. Like musical instruments of
marvellous construction, we are so strung that
the air which causes vibration, seems to breathe
but in the music, and one string is no sooner
struck than all awake in harmony. And we are
attuned to each other so perfectly, that under
similar circumstances of health, being free from
the dull pressure of care, all humanity will perhaps respond to one heart.

But the science and execution of music affords
us still better illustration. How nice a structure
must be called into play when a skilful pianist, by
aid of an additional instrument fitted to his convenience, executes an intricate piece of music, not
only in a wonderfully rapid succession of mechanical movements, but also in a manner fully to
express the very feelings of his soul! But how
much more forcibly is the same power manifested
in the human voice! By it the spirit speaks not
only an infinite variety of articulated sounds, but
more marvellously still by the modulated language
of tones, so as to excite into extacy or agony,
every sympathy within us.

What is it that so skilfully touches this instrument? What is it that enjoys as well as actuates, receives as well as communicates, through this inscrutable organization? It is as we have said the soul or spirit, without which this body were more unmeaning than a statue, and only fit, as it would tend, to decay. It is the soul which animates the features and causes them to present a living picture of each passion, so that the inmost agitations of the heart become visible in a moment, and the wish that would seek concealment betrays its presence and its power, in the vivid eye, while the blood kindles into crimson with a thought that burns along the brow. It is this which diffuses a sweet serenity and rest upon the visage, when our feelings are tranquillized, and our thoughts abide with heaven, like ocean in a calm, reflecting the peaceful glories of the cloudless skies. This indwelling spirit of power blends our features into unison and harmony, and awakes "the music breathing from the face," when in association with those we love, and heart answering to heart, we live in sympathy, while memory and hope repose alike in smiles upon the bosom of enjoyment. It is a flame from heaven purer than Promethean fire, that vivifies and energizes the breathing form. It is an immaterial essence, a being, that quickens matter and imparts life, sensation, motion, to the intricate framework of our bodies; which wills when we act, attends when we perceive, looks into the past when we reflect, and not content with the present, shoots with all its aims and all its hopes into the futurity that is for ever dawning upon it.

CHAPTER II.

THE ORGANS OF SENSE ARE THE INSTRUMENTS OF THE MIND.

PROBABLY none but uncreated mind can act without being acted on, at least facts appear to demonstrate that the human spirit has no originating power, but is moved only as it is impressed by circumstances and extraneous influences. Hence the necessity of its being supplied with instruments and senses, organized in keeping with the sphere which it inhabits, in order that its capacity for action might be elicited and manifested by agents appropriate to its innate functions and endowments.

We are accustomed to say the eye sees, the ear hears, the finger feels, and so forth, but such language is incorrect, and only admissible because we are accustomed to the error, and our expressions are necessarily accommodated to ignorance, or are not equal to our knowledge. The eye itself no more sees, than the telescope which we hold before it to assist our vision. The ear hears not any more than the trumpet of tin, which the deaf

c

man directs towards the speaker to convey the
sound of his voice, and so with regard to all the
organs of sense. They are but instruments which
become the *media* of intelligence to the absolute
mind, which uses them, whenever that mind is
inclined or obliged to employ them. Or, perhaps,
they might be more correctly represented as the
seats and proper places of impressions, because of
their exact adaptation to external influences. They
bear such relations to the condition of the materials which surround us, as, in the healthy state
of their functions, always to present true and real
intimations of circumstances within the range of
their faculty or formation.

The slightest examination of the organs of sense
will, however, convince an observer that they are
constructed merely as instruments. What is the
eye but a most perfect optical contrivance? It
is composed of the best materials, arranged in the
best manner, for the purpose of rendering illuminated objects not only visible, but tangible, for
sight can be demonstrated to be a finer sort of
feeling, the colours which represent distance and
shape, being brought in contact with the nerve,
and with that which perceives in the nerve. The
cornea is a most perfect convex glass, set distinctly in its proper place and proper manner,
with the same design, but with far greater precision than the optician sets his crystal to aid the

sight. The various translucent membranes, the lens, the humours of different densities, and even the blood, abruptly made transparent in its passage, and much besides, too minute to be now mentioned, conspire to transmit and duly refract, and regulate the rays of light, so that they may fall upon the exact point, and there present to the observant spirit, a perfect picture of the majestic, the beautiful, the glorious; and bring into our being those impressions which preserve our interest and sympathy with universal nature. No mechanism invented by man, was ever so well contrived or so well placed, or could move so precisely as required under the action of its pulleys. No servant was ever so obedient; for, without a conscious effort of the will, without a command, and as if instinct with the mind that employs it, this exquisite apparatus, which is both a camera-obscura and a telescope, instantaneously takes the direction of a desire and accommodates itself to the range of distance, and the degree of light.

And the ear is a complete acoustic instrument, with its exterior trumpet to collect sounds, and its vibrating tympanum, and its chamber and winding passages, and its dense fluids, so well calculated to propagate and modify vibrations, and its minute and sensitive muscles, to act as cords to brace the drum, just as required, and to move the jointed piston, which regulates the water in its canals, according to circumstances, and the whole built up within a stone-like structure, which prevents the sound from being wasted.   There is much of wisdom in the arrangement of this wonderful living instrument, as indeed in others also, the meaning of which human sagacity cannot discover, but this much however can always be ascertained, the purpose is to bring the mind into contact with that which it would know.

The senses moreover correspond together, and thus enable the mind to correct the impressions of one by those of the others, in such a manner as, by their united operation to obtain full and accurate intelligence concerning the surrounding world.

The well-known case which the philosophic Cheselden has related, affords a decisive experiment, agreeing as it does with many others, in proof that the information derived from the sense of sight requires to be corrected by information from different sources, but that when the habit of seeing is established under this correction, vision continues to suggest the true relations of objects to each other.

A young gentleman, who had no remembrance of ever having seen, was couched and received his sight, but when he first saw he could not judge of distances, but thought all visible objects touched his eye, as what he felt touched his skin.   He expected that pictures would feel like what they represented, and was amazed when he found those parts which by light and shadow appeared round and uneven, felt flat like the rest, and asked which was the lying sense, feeling or sight. When shewn a miniature of his father, he acknowledged the likeness, but desired to know how it could be that so large a face, could be expressed in so small a compass, saying it seemed as impossible to him as to put a bushel into a pint. The things he first saw he thought extremely large, and upon seeing larger things, those first seen he conceived less, not being able to imagine any lines beyond the bounds he beheld. He could not conceive that the house could look larger than the room he was in. He said every new object was a new delight. On first beholding a large prospect his pleasure was beyond expression, and he called it a new kind of seeing.

These details prove, that sight does not originally inform us respecting the real distance or magnitude of objects, but that we learn these things from the experience and help of our other senses; therefore the mind exercises an independent judgment in comparing their impressions, a power which the senses themselves could never have conferred.

CHAPTER III.

THE MIND IS NOT THE RESULT OF SENSATION.

THERE is a disposition to exercise the senses from the enjoyment afforded by the act, but this disposition of course resides, not in the organs, but in the mind, being the result of our mental constitution, in connection with nerves through which we discover suitable objects. The mind is excited by whatever is appropriate to it, and the senses are stimulated in sympathy with the mind, because they are its organs, the means of action and enjoyment. Whatever pleases the mind the senses seek: the eye, light; the ear, modulated sound; the smell, fragrance; the taste, flavour; the touch, degrees of pressure; and the muscles possess an agreeable sense of their own, arising probably from their power of adjusting the body for the accommodation of the mind, in the exercise of the senses generally.

What is meant by this adjustment will appear when we reflect on the machinery which is consentaneously set in motion in the act of using either of the senses, but more especially perhaps sight and touch.   It is not enough that the sensation of a visible object should be present in the eye; in order to look so as to examine an object, it is also necessary that the will be exerted.   The first sensation of an object only serves as a stimulus to the appetite of the mind, to rouse its attention, and excite the will, which, acting on the muscles, prepares the eye for further scrutiny, and at the same time places all the body in keeping with the state and desire of the mind, so that we can generally see from the attitude of a person how his eye is engaged.

The muscular consent between the eye and the rest of the body, particularly the hand, is well shewn in fencing, where every movement is guided not by looking to see how the weapon should be directed, but by fixing your eye on your antagonist's eye: his intention there expressed, and acting as it were through your own eye on your nervous system, causes an instantaneous and instinctive adjustment of your body accordingly. The same thing is exhibited also in the precision with which the savage hunter learns to direct his arrow, and the politer sportsman to point his gun.

Here let us enquire—does organization produce the consciousness of self? No; for we feel organization to be distinct from ourselves. The child just beginning to use its senses, never confounds the objects of sense with itself, and its own body is but one of these objects. The individual soul, which, by experience and suitable organs, manifests intellect or mind, not only perceives the sensations and interprets them according to past experience, but it has an influence in modifying their impressions, and intensifying their effects according to certain laws which regulate its connection with the senses.

Mind has the power of distinguishing sensations and of causing one sense to be employed in preference to another, and, to a certain extent, of correcting the impressions made on them all. The brain, connecting the senses together, enables the mind to employ them in relation to each other, and to compare sensation with sensation as regards time, space, and degree of force; so that whatever interrupts or disturbs the regular function of this connecting medium of all sense, the brain, necessarily causes the mind to perceive and to compare, in a disordered manner, as in delirium, insanity, and idiotism, or else the brain becomes so diseased that it altogether ceases to convey impressions from without, and thus perchance allows the mind to proceed in its activity with the consciousness of past ideas which it continues to combine, according to the laws of its being, perhaps irrespective of physical association.

However necessary the intelligence derived from

the senses may be, to the development of mental capacity in this state of existence, it is yet evident that mind is not the result of sensation, nor, as to the origin of its peculiar faculties, at all dependent on the power of the senses, for in order to use them aright and to obtain correct impressions through them, there must exist inherently, and antecedently an ability in the mind or thinking principle, to attend and to compare. What is experience but the amount of impressions received by the mind? It contributes nothing to the mental improvement, but as the mind possesses the power of judging; a power which no experience can itself confer, any more than the objects presented can produce the will that chooses between them.

It is the prerogative of the thinking soul, to learn by observation; that is, to employ the senses and to judge by analogy. But this implies that a reasoning being is attending as soon as the senses are brought into exercise, and that it is prepared to work as soon as it finds materials to work with. Facts prove the truth of this position. According to the nature of the mind residing in any body,—supposing of course the body in health and fitted for it,—so will be the exhibition of that mind. Its experience can never alter its nature. The education of the senses can never create a new mind. A brute can

c 3

acquire no notion of moral truth by training,
but a human soul is always rational, and from its
earliest manifestation in the body, always reasons
or infers correctly according to the extent of its
knowledge. "The child is father of the man."
Though the senses which it uses are no better
than a brute's, how vastly superior the result of
their employment! The human being sees intuitively beyond sense, and venerates the unknown
which the known indicates; and while experience
administers to hope, chooses not merely according
to appetite, but to conviction, for what he believes
determines his actions; and as his reason consents
to truth, without demanding any other demonstration than its fitness, so he lives in the enjoyment of what he expects as well as in what he
realizes.

We must live by faith. We must trust though
we know that our senses often deceive us; we must
still rely, for our perceptions of sensible objects
depends on them. Moreover we naturally believe
what cannot be demonstrated to our senses, for
reason and conscience rest on convictions derived
from a higher source.

There is a correspondence or consent between
the mind and the nerves of sensation. The nerves
being disordered, false impressions are received.
Experience may correct them but it often happens
that she is incompetent, or the defect may have

been congenital, then the mind manifests itself in a defective manner, and is said to be either idiotic or insane. The due relation between the senses and the soul, the link that connects them is broken, and the thinking principle continues to act according to the power of the machinery with which it is associated, and according to its innate energy and consciousness. If that part of the nervous system be diseased in which the impressions of sense combine, that is the central brain, then the faculties of attention and comparison are of course interfered with, or prevented from acting in proper order, and the individual so afflicted is insane. This disorder being removed, the man is restored to his senses; for the mind itself cannot be insane, but it is always able to act aright with a correct organization, or when there is no interference to disturb its functions. How far the mind may be wilfully perverted, and attracted from the truth it knows, and thus become what may be called morally insane, will perhaps appear as we proceed.

That the indwelling mind is ever ready to act in connection with a proper state of nerve, is beautifully exhibited in many cases of recovery from partial idiotism, in which the faculties and affections have lain dormant from infancy, till some circumstance has altered the state of the brain so as to bring the mind into its proper relation with the exterior world, and enable it to manifest the wonderful endowments of reason by observing and comparing.

Probably in cases of idiotism, sensation is confused as well as the reflective faculties. There is an unsteadiness in the use of the senses, and an indeterminateness not unlike what we witness in persons who are overpowered by accumulated nervous excitement. It is manifestly a disease of the nerves, a disorder in the instruments of sensation, which hinders the mind from attending and correctly applying them. Hence the soulless countenance, the rude mixture of instincts and passions, the unmeaning mirth, the transient fear, the gustly violence. This confusion of faculties and feelings has sometimes been reduced to order even in hereditary idiotism. Light has touched the chaos into beauty; a slight interference has awakened the torpid soul; an accident has removed the obstruction between the intellect and the world: a fracture of the skull, a fit of frenzy, a fever has cured the disease, and the idiot has suddenly become an observant, reasoning man. Beings whose rudimentary senses seemed incapable of obedience to will, too restless to allow the soul proper intercourse with external nature, without moral sentiments, without affections,— mere instinctive animals, without associates in creation, yet possessing some unimaginable happiness in their own confused sensations and propensities,—even such imbecile and worse than brutal enormities have, by the philosophic and Christian philanthropist, been brought into relation to other beings, redeemed from the dominion of disgusting appetites, and caused to seek intelligent enjoyment in loving and pleasing their instructors and friends. Many such idiots have been thus rendered visibly and mentally human by the skilful patience with which M. Voisin, at the Bicêtre, Paris, has employed means to attract their attention to an associating succession of objects. If, then, the prison of the spirit has by such causes been converted into its pleasant palace, what shall hinder the soul of an idiot from enjoying at death its emancipation from the impeding body and its entrance on a commodious abode. Surely the intelligent principle within them requires only to be put into proper relation with the world it inhabits to develope its capacity for knowledge and happiness.

The same important truth is demonstrated in those instances in which some deficiency in the organization of the senses has shut up the soul from the enjoyment of its appropriate objects, as in the cases of deaf mutes. And is not ignorance deaf, blind, dumb, unfeeling? And is not education the quickener of the soul, enabling it to burst from the grave to see, taste, handle the things of life?

What a delightful and heavenly occupation is it to set at large an immortal spirit from silent, speechless, dark, imprisonment! How ecstatic the interest to watch the gladdening being gradually liberated from its living tomb, and brought into rapturous sympathy with other souls! The person who can peruse Dr. Howe's narrative of Laura Bridgman's case without emotion, such as a father feels in regarding his own new-born child, which he loves because created in his own likeness, is not a Christian, and has not yet had a glimpse of the vision which reveals the beauty and value of a human spirit.

CHAPTER IV.

ILLUSTRATIONS OF THE VALUE OF THE SENSES AND OBSERVATIONS ON THEIR USE.

LAURA BRIDGMAN was completely deprived of sight and hearing at an early period of childhood. She was born in Hanover, New Hampshire, on the 21st December, 1829. Doctor Howe, her great benefactor and friend, has published an exceedingly interesting narrative, from which, or rather from that part of it given in Dickens' "American Notes," the following paragraphs are extracted: "As soon as she could walk she began to explore the room and the house; she became familiar with the form, density, weight and heat of every article she could lay her hands upon. She followed her mother, and felt her hands and arms as she was occupied about the house; and her disposition to imitate led her to repeat everything herself; she even learned to sew a little and to knit. At this time I was so fortunate as to hear of the child, and immediately hastened to Hanover to see her, I found her with a well-formed figure; a strongly marked nervous-sanguine temperament, a large and beautifully shaped head; and the whole system in healthy action. The parents were easily induced to consent to her coming to Boston, and on the 4th October, 1837, they brought her to the institution. After waiting about two weeks, the attempt was made to give her knowledge of arbitrary signs, by which she could interchange thoughts with others. There was one of two ways to be adopted; either to go on to build up a language of signs which she had already commenced herself, or to teach her the purely arbitrary language in common use; that is, to give her a sign for every individual thing, or to give her a knowledge of letters by combination of which she might express her idea of the existence, and the mode and condition of existence, of anything. The former would have been easy but very ineffectual, the latter seemed very difficult, but, if accomplished, very effectual. I determined therefore to try the latter."

After describing the interesting process by which he taught her to associate names with things, he goes on to say " Hitherto the process had been mechanical, and the success about as great as teaching a knowing dog a variety of tricks. The poor child had sat in mute amazement, and patiently imitated everything her teacher did; but now the truth began to flash upon her; her intellect began to work; she perceived that here was

a way by which she could herself make up a sign
of anything that was in her own mind, and shew
it to another mind, and at once her countenance
lighted up with a human expression; it was no
longer a dog, or a parrot; it was an immortal
spirit, eagerly seizing upon a new link of union
with other spirits!   I could almost fix upon the
·moment when the truth first dawned upon her
mind, and spread its light to her countenance;
I saw that the great obstacle was overcome; and
that henceforward nothing but patient and per-
severing, but plain and straightforward efforts
were to be used."

At the end of the year a report of the case was
made of which the following is an extract.   "It
has been ascertained, beyond the possibility of
doubt, that she cannot see a ray of light, cannot
hear the least sound, and never exercises her
sense of smell if she has any.   Thus her mind
dwells in darkness and stillness, as profound as
that of a closed tomb at midnight.   Of beautiful
sights and sweet sounds, and pleasant odours she
has no conception, nevertheless she is as happy
and playful as a bird, or a lamb, and the employment of her intellectual faculties, or the acquirement of a new idea, gives her a vivid pleasure,
which is plainly marked in her expressive features."

Describing the interesting process by which he
taught her to associate names with things, he

goes on to say, "If she have no occupation she
evidently amuses herself by imaginary dialogues,
or by recalling past impressions; she counts with
her fingers, or spells out names of things which
she has recently learned, in the manual alphabet
of the deaf mutes. In this lonely self-commu-
nion, she seems to reason, reflect, and argue.
But wonderful as is the rapidity with which she·
writes her thoughts upon the air, still more so is
the ease and rapidity with which she reads the
words thus written by another; grasping their
hands in hers, and following every movement of
their fingers, as letter after letter conveys their
meaning to her mind. It is in this way that she
converses with her blind playmates, and nothing
can more forcibly show the power of mind in forc-
ing matter to its purpose, than a meeting between
them. For if great skill and talent are necessary
for two pantomimes to paint their thoughts and
feelings by the movements of the body and the
expression of the countenance, how much greater
the difficulty when darkness shrouds them both,
and the one can hear no sound! When Laura is
walking through a passage-way with her hands
spread before her, she knows instantly every one
she meets, and passes them with a sign of recognition, but if it be a girl of her own age, and especially if it be one of her favourites, there is
instantly a bright smile of recognition and a twin-

ing of arms, a grasping of hands, and a swift telegraph upon the tiny fingers."

Her mother came to visit her and the scene of their meeting was an interesting one. "The mother stood sometime gazing with overflowing eyes, upon her unfortunate child, who, all unconscious of her presence, was playing about the room. Presently Laura ran against her, and at once began feeling her hands, examining her dress, and trying to find out if she knew her, but not succeeding in this she turned away as from a stranger, and the poor woman could not conceal the pang she felt, at finding that her beloved child did not know her. She then gave Laura a string of beads which she used to wear at home, which were recognized by the child at once, who with much joy put them round her neck and sought me eagerly, to say that she understood the string was from her home. The mother now tried to caress her, but poor Laura repelled her, preferring to be with her acquaintances. Another article from home was now given her, and she began to look much interested. After a while, on her mother taking hold of her again, a vague idea seemed to flit across Laura's mind that this could not be a stranger; she therefore felt her hands very eagerly, while her countenance assumed an expression of intense interest; she became very pale and then suddenly red; hope seemed struggling with doubt and anxiety, and never were contending emotions more strongly painted upon the human face. At this moment of painful uncertainty, the mother drew her close to her side and kissed her fondly, when at once the truth flashed upon the child, and all mistrust and anxiety disappeared from her face, as with an expression of exceeding joy, she eagerly nestled to the bosom of her parent, and yielded herself to her fond embrace."

The subsequent parting between them showed alike the affection, the intelligence, and the resolution of the child. Laura accompanied her mother to the door clinging close to her all the way, until they arrived at the threshold, where she paused and felt around to ascertain who was near her. Perceiving the matron, of whom she is very fond, she grasped her with one hand, holding on convulsively to her mother with the other, and thus she stood for a moment; then she dropped her mother's hand, put her handkerchief to her eyes, and turning round, clung sobbing to the matron, while her mother departed with emotions as deep as those of her child.

She is fond of having other children noticed and caressed by the teachers, and those whom she respects; but this must not be carried on too far or she becomes jealous. She wants to have her share, which, if not the lion's, is the greater part; and if she does not get it, she will say, *" My mother will love me."* Her tendency to imitation is so strong, that it leads her to actions which must be entirely incomprehensible to her, and which can give her no other pleasure than *the gratification of an internal faculty*. She has been known to sit, for half an hour, holding a book before her sightless eyes, and moving her lips, as she (by the help of her fingers) has observed other people do when reading. Her social feelings and her affections are very strong; and when she is sitting at work, or at her studies by the side of one of her little friends, she will break off from her task every few moments and hug and kiss them with an earnestness and warmth that is touching to behold. When left alone she occupies and apparently amuses herself, and seems quite contented; and so strong seems to be the natural tendency of thought to put on the garb of language, that she often soliloquizes in the *finger language,* slow and tedious as it is. But it is only when alone, that she is quiet; for if she becomes sensible of the presence of any one near her, she is restless until she can sit close beside them, hold their hand, and converse with them by signs. In her intellectual character it is pleasing to observe an insatiable thirst for knowledge, and a quick perception of the relations of things. In her moral character it is beautiful to behold her continual

gladness, her keen enjoyment of existence, her
expansive love, her unhesitating. confidence, her
sympathy with suffering, her conscientiousness,
truthfulness, and hopefulness."

So long a quotation may need an apology, especially as the work from which it has been taken
is of a popular kind and extensively read.   A
mere allusion however to facts which so powerfully illustrate the subject of this work would not
suffice, and an abridgement would be an injus-
tice.   Neither Dr. Howe nor the reader can desire
the curtailment of so triumphant a story, which
affords something very like a demonstration not
only that the mind depends not entirely on the
senses for its powers, but also that it possesses a
distinct existence and calls "the body mine not
me." Laura clearly evinces a moral perception of
right and wrong which could not have been taught
her but through an innate moral consciousness.
Indeed moral feeling cannot in any person have
sprung from mere conventional knowledge, but
from a consenting faculty independent on education, acknowledging the fitness or unfitness, propriety or impropriety, of any act in relation of
mind to mind.   She was fond of having other
children noticed and caressed.   She felt the worth
of love that delights in the happiness of associates,
and she appreciated others by the kindness which
their conduct evinced towards herself.   She thus

acknowledged the true law of heaven, written on her heart, not by man's teaching but by the finger of God.   She could feel the force of the royal commandment *"Do unto others as you would they should do to you,"* and needed only to know the truth in order to approve it, because of its felt fitness to her moral nature and her relationship to other beings.   There can be no reason therefore that she should be without religious feelings. The true object of veneration can be presented to her apprehension and that not merely as regards her conceptions of infinite power and duration, but also as to the moral attributes.   At least she could be made to understand her own sentiment in a higher sense, and be as ready to say, "God loves me" as that her mother loves her.   Dr. Fowler, of Salisbury, suggests that she might be taught the idea of infinity by her idea of estimating distance, and of eternity by time.   Certainly imagination would oppose no barrier to the questions—why should not this measure be prolonged without end? why not this consciousness last for ever?   Here then we have through the same reason, the sublimest conception of a Newton engrafted on the soul of a deaf, blind, speechless girl, taught by the nature of her own feelings and affections what materialists dare not claim for any arrangement of matter—Infinite power and Eternal love!

Several illustrative and striking instances of a similar kind are recorded. Dugal Stewart read an interesting paper before the Royal Society concerning a man fifty years of age, named James Mitchell. He was without speech, sight and hearing, but not without affections. His sister could communicate her wishes to him, and the wilfulness of his impetuous disposition yielded with the docility of a little child to the touch of her loving hand. His soul seems to have created a diversified world of its own out of two elements, for by feeling and smell alone he acquired his sublime knowledge. These, his only senses, were spiritually acute, because he intently observed their intimations, and they furnished him with almost supernatural intelligence. He evidently inferred from feeling more than is commonly derived from that faculty, and experienced exquisite delight, as his actions expressed, from testing the many tangible properties of bodies within his reach. His curiosity was unbounded, and his invention fertile. He knelt at family prayers as if he fully understood the meaning of the attitude. And does it not necessarily express humility and hope? Would not the bending of the knees, and the lifting up of the hands, and the quiet waiting, have indicated to him the idea of dependence on some present but yet intangible power from whom his own being was derived? Our very frame-work,

properly employed, teaches us of God's power
and goodness, and the act of assuming a devout
attitude is perhaps necessarily associated with re-
verential ideas, as the result of a natural law of
our physiological and mental existence, as long as
our minds are not possessed by impure ideas. The
position of weakness and want is an appeal to
Omnipotence, and we feel it to be so.

This man heard the voice of God in his heart,
more distinctly than many who receive the word
of life and immortality with the outward ear;
and this word was visible to the sight of his
soul although his eye drank not the light. He
shrunk back in horror from the corpse of his father, for he recognized death, and never would
rest in the room where the dead body had been
laid, but sometime afterwards he took a stranger
into the apartment, placed his hand a moment on
the pillow where his father's head had rested,
hurried his companion to the grave, and patted it
with his hand. This could not have been the expression of his hopelessness, but of his unbroken
relationship to a living father, and of his expectation of life beyond the tomb.

All the facts concerning the use of the senses
demonstrate, in short, that the soul possesses
intuitive endowments which the senses could not
confer, for the faculty of using them is mental,
and must of course precede their use. Our senses

D

are constituted for this world and we enjoy it;
our undeveloped spirits are constituted in correspondence with another world and we shall enter it.

> " Even so the soul in this contracted state,
> Confined to these straight instruments of sense,
> More dull and narrowly doth operate;
> At this hole hears, the sight may ray from thence,
> Here tastes, there smells; but when she's gone from hence,
> Like naked lamp she is one shining sphere,
> And round about hath perfect cognizance,
> Whatever in her horizon doth appear,
> She is one orb of sense : all eye, all touch, all ear."
>
> MOOR, 1650.

The practical inference from facts concerning
the use of our senses is simply the propriety of
taking care to employ them suitably, to preserve
and improve them, since our social comfort and
influence as well as our intellectual advancement
depend in this world on their integrity. Their
destruction is the exclusion of knowledge and
wisdom at their only entrances. Delicacy of perception is essential to acuteness of intellect, but
perception is perfected rather by the power and
habit of attention in the use of the senses than by
keenness of sensation.

After reading such beautiful narratives as that
of Laura Bridgman, how easy is it to imagine a
human spirit untainted by the loveless experiences of this selfish world, and released from a

body so stamped with the physical image of in-
herited moral disorder as to be incapable of any
distinct idea. We can imagine the soul of an
idiot for instance set free from the body, the tomb
in which Omnipotence had interred it, only the
better to show forth His glory. Doubtless many
a maternal heart that loves the mature idiot, as
the babe nestled in helplessness on the bosom, is
cheered by this thought. We may watch its entrance into a world of light, beauty, and love;
there to be educated by angels instead of a man,
even though such as he who trained Laura Bridgman, and who seemed indeed to have been actuated by a feeling of angelic purpose and charity.
How rapid the progress of this unshackled soul in
divine learning! How rapturous its joy at the
wonders of wisdom everywhere visible! how un-
utterable the fulness of its sympathy with heavenly
affections! And what human child is not capable
of the same expansion amidst the genial influences
of heaven, though here it may have been shut up
in a body unfit for mind, or left at its birth apparently to perish. The spirit was there struggling
for mastery. , The germ of immortality was in it,
and that seed shall live and grow, in spite of visible death and decay, far above the evil that would
cling about its first tendencies to take root in this
earth's accursed soil.

By thus simply gazing in fancy on a naked soul

we see a ray of light opening into eternity; we
seem to get a glimpse at all the reconciling possibilities which we so much need to explain to us the
reason of our present mysterious and incongruous
existence.   But imagination would reveal a vision
too vast and glorious for our present sight.   What
is possible we must not enquire.   What we know
not now we shall know hereafter.   Facts present
are intended to instruct us, and if we duly observe
them they will be ours for ever, and we shall trace
their connexion with futurity. Rational inferences
from facts are not however mere airy surmises,
but solid truths; and every expectation, fairly
founded on experience, is of the nature of true
prophecy, being consistent with the universal reason by which all events are ordered.   Hence the
propriety of investigation, and hence the foreseeing sagacity which really scientific and truthful
inquiry always confers.   Hence also the strength
of true religious convictions, and the assurance,
the evidence, of things not seen,—the substance
and reality of things hoped for. Any single truth,
followed up in all its relations, connects us with
all other truth.   Like the light, however various
its manifestations, it is one in its nature, and it
emanates from one source, to which it necessarily
conducts the eye of all who will look off from the
objects it illuminates to the fountain of light itself.
Since truths are thus connected in one system,

facts can never lead reason astray. She has power
to examine evidence and will not receive into her
belief any notion which is incompatible with analogy. Not to compare impression with experience,
is not to reason, but to act like a certain naval
officer, holding a very responsible situation, who
was very fond of making telescopic observations.
Among other strange things he solemnly asserted,
that when Napoleon abdicated in 1814, he saw the
Emperor's figure in the sun. The next day the
figure appeared like a skeleton, and on the third
day the united colours of the allies had taken its
place. These appearances were regularly entered
in the log-book, and several of the crew were
ready to testify to the accuracy of the Captain's
observations. Such facts only prove that the
mind may be so deceived by its own desires as to
employ the senses to confirm its errors. Reason
then is a better and more certain guide than the
senses. She enables us to discern the folly of
believing according to sight. She looks deeper
than the superficies of things, and enjoys the
consciousness of realities belonging to a region
too bright for any eye but her own to gaze on.
She needs no telescope nor credulous witnesses to
confirm her faith in those truths which dwell in
the light she is accustomed to contemplate, and
which are commended to the mind of man by
their fitness to promote his advancement in know-

ledge, virtue and happiness. Had not man the
faculty of perceiving truths beyond the sphere of
sense he would be no better than an irresponsible
brute, and the fact that man infers and travels
on in reason beyond material things is itself a
proof that his mind is not material.

CHAPTER V.

THE CONNEXION OF THE MIND WITH THE BRAIN, &c.

A few words concerning the definite nature of matter will conduct us to a consideration of the connexion of the mind with the brain.

The divisibility of matter has led to curious discussion, some saying that if matter cannot be divided and subdivided without end and still remain possessed of dimensions, etc., then it must either become spirit or be annihilated. Such a notion of matter is absurd, for it involves the belief of one of three impossibilities: the conversion of brute matter into a thinking principle, its withdrawal from existence, or its capability of being divided infinitely, that is, that every imaginary particle of matter may be still divided into as many parts as there are moments in eternity! Such reasoners seem to forget that the properties of matter are imposed by Omnipotence. The will of His wisdom limits all things, even the exercise of His own power. Those materialists who have lost all idea of Deity in their study of the physical world, might have

learned a different conclusion even from the law
of chemical combination, by which the elements
unite to each other in certain proportions.   Matter must have been made in definite atoms, or
how should different chemical elements always
combine by weight and measure, in exact order
and proportion,—so much of one to so much of
another, and in no other manner?   The reason
of this universal fact we can understand, when
we conceive that so many definite atoms of one
element combine with so many definite atoms of
another.   If there be not definite atoms, how
can there be definite combinations ?

It has also been said, that God could cause
matter to think.   Who can say yes?   He has
not made us capable of thinking so.   We cannot
conceive of such matter, for the words thought
and matter always present inconvertible and con-
tradictory ideas ; because our rational consciousness assures us that thought has no analogy to
any known property of matter.

The mental unity, which each man calls *I*,
cannot exist as a part of the body; for what part
can we suppose to be a unit, either in structure,
function, or substance ?   The soul, being one,
"spreads undivided, operates unspent," and confers a kind of unity upon the organization which
it employs, by the act of using it for one purpose
at a time.   It is but one will that enforces the

obedience of the body, therefore no diversity or division in the organization can destroy the impression of our unity in volition and feeling. "If joy or sorrow," observes Dr. Brown, "be an affection of the brain, it is an affection of various substances, which, though distinct in their own existences, we comprehend under this single term. If the affection therefore be common to the whole, it is not one joy or sorrow, but a number of joys and sorrows, corresponding with the number of separate particles thus affected; which, if matter be infinitely divisible, may be divided into an infinite number of little joys or sorrows, that have no other relation to each other than the relations of proximity, by which they may be grouped together in spheres and cubes, or other solids, regular or irregular, of pleasures or pains; but by which it is impossible for them to become one pleasure or pain."

There are several reasons for believing that the mind is not confined to the brain, such as the propagation of the lower species of animals by spontaneous division, each separate part having a distinct will and special desires. Then again in the generation of man,—the germ and fecundating fluid, being productions of separate individuals, when brought together produce a new individual in the likeness of the parents. Hence the mental principle, if it be propagated and not rather added to life, when this is developed in certain organizations, must exist in other parts of the body besides the brain, and be capable of continuing in a latent state. If then the mental principle be not limited to the brain, it follows that the destruction of the brain does not necessarily destroy the mind, but only prevents its ordinary manifestation; and if it be something superadded to the body, there is no reason why it should not exist with all its thoughts out of the body.

M. Flourens's experiments are too numerous and extensive to quote, but they prove that the brain may be destroyed to a large extent, in any direction, without destroying any of its functions; but when the nervous mass, connecting the organs of the senses and their sympathies together, is divided, the manifestation of mind is interrupted. It follows inevitably from his experiments, that the faculty of perceiving and desiring one object operates on the same organ as the faculty of perceiving and comparing any other object, and therefore the different affections are not functions of different parts of the brain, as some phrenologists assert, but of that which uses the brain under various states of impression, according to its individual nature and experience.

In mental derangement,—attention, judgment, memory, volition, are always more or less disordered; and yet in the common phrenological systems these are not represented in any part of the brain, nor can be; therefore these essential principles of mental action must be something more than functions of the brain. As far as I can discover, by examination of a multitude of recorded cases,—attention, judgment, memory, and volition, may be all freely exercised by persons in whom many of the organs appropriated by phrenologists to the intellect are destroyed or disordered by disease; but these operations of mind become deranged whenever the nervous centre is rendered incapable of performing its function, in energizing the body, so as to hinder the mind from putting itself and the senses into proper relation to external influences and to each other; therefore I infer that mental insanity, and even what we call unconsciousness, are only the results of physical impediment to the united and associated action of nerve under the operation of mind, which is benevolently constituted to be manifested to other minds only in connexion with a certain state of organization.

Insanity, like certain dreams, seems generally to be a kind of confusion, arising from a mixture of memory with present impressions. The consciousness, or the sense of each of the two states that belong to the mind, is not kept perfectly distinct as it is in the sound condition of the brain, but the attention is divided between remembered ideas and sensible realities, the one being mistaken for the other. Of course it is the same individual being which perceives the idea as it exists in the mind, as a remembered thing, and also the present impression conveyed at the moment through either of the senses.

One of the outrageous consequences of receiving the vulgar phrenological doctrines in their full extravagance has been, an attempt to prove, on scientific principles, that the soul itself is double because the organs of the body are. But we have seen that the unity of the mind is not broken in consequence of its connexion with a plurality of organs, and surely it as easily reasons from the impressions of two brains as it sees with two eyes. That the two grand divisions of the brains are practically, as well as anatomically, two brains, is proved by a number of cases in which memory and the other functions of the mind have been exercised without apparent impairment, in persons who have had one hemisphere so destroyed by disease as to leave no portion of its substance in a natural state.

Tiedemann relates the case of a lunatic, who was insane on one side of his head, and who observed and corrected his insanity with the other. Now it may be asked, who observed and corrected the insanity? The man certainly, not one half of him. No doubt the diseased brain could not be employed without occasioning disordered manifestation of mind; and, of course, as long as the other half of his brain was awake and obedient to the will, he could perceive and rebuke the dreamy absurdities connected with the other. He compared the diseased perception and action with the healthy, and felt at once which was consistent with waking experience; and therefore, by the bye, he could have been but half a lunatic at the worst, and that only when the sound part of his head was awake. Such cases, after all, scarcely differ from those in which individuals consciously labour under illusions of sense, and are able to rectify false impressions by comparison with true.

To argue from the duality of the organs, that the mind, which is manifested through them, is also dual, is really the same as to argue that two minds are employed to see with two eyes or hear with two ears. But consciousness is never double, and attention is never divided. Transition from thought to thought and subject to subject, may be more rapid than the light, but yet it is the act of one and the same mind, to pass from thought to thought, comparing one with another, and drawing conclusions according to experience. The mind has doubtless double dealing enough in the midst of its mixed motives and clashing in-

terests; but if we are to infer from hence that
there are two minds, it will puzzle the judge to
determine which mind is at fault and to be pun-
ished when the double-minded man commits a
murder; for surely one half of him, at least, and
probably the more perfect, is innocent. How
unjust to hang a whole man for the will of only
one side of him. Alas! the ingenious plea will
never save him, for common sense is single.
Surely it is a very one-sided reasoning which
reduces a man of science thus to do things by
halves, and divide the responsibility between his
two volitions. It is to be feared that morality
and religion will slip between them and find a
place in neither. Bishop Taylor shall pass sentence on this subject: "He that will pretend
anything that is beyond ordinary, as he that will
say that he has two reasonable souls, or three
wills, is not to be confuted but with physic, or by
tying him to abjure his folly till he were able to
prove it."

Acuteness of faculty depends on the power of
maintaining attention; but this power is interfered
with by any disorder of the nervous system, because attention itself is an act of the mind, by
which the nervous system is put into a condition
to obey the soul, to receive impressions from without, or to operate on muscle. The purpose for
which we possess a duality of organization appears

then to be, that we may be able to attend the longer without fatigue and confusion; for we rest the one side while employing the other. If, therefore, we are deprived of the use of an eye, for instance, we the sooner find the other to fail, unless it be the more sparingly engaged. This principle is perhaps the secret of sympathy between the two sides of our bodies. Probably the duality of the brain serves a purpose similar to that of the duality of the senses. In some relations to the mind, the double arrangement enables us to continue thinking or acting consecutively for a longer time than would otherwise be possible: the one rests while the other acts, and so on alternately, until both alike demand the repose and refreshment to be obtained only by sleep.

CHAPTER VI.

EVILS OF POPULAR PHRENOLOGY.

THE dangerous tendency of the popular notions of phrenology, is most evident in the excuses it supplies to those who seek apologies for their moral depravity, and in the impediments it builds up in the way of those inquisitive minds that expect to find in nature a substitute for revelation. Many, convinced of the authority of the Bible, yet seem to see so much of demonstration in this pseudo-science at variance with the declarations of that strong book, that they are constantly hanging in suspense between the ruling faith, in the spiritual origin of thought, and the vacillating persuasion of the material beginning and end of mind. With such persons, morality and Christianity are thus at stake. A thorough, uncompromising, common phrenologist must apologize if he exhibit respect for either divine or human government; since a will that owns no source but in the accidents of a man's organization, can have no relation to the law which demands obedience for the common good. What good can there be to a mind unassociated, and indeed not existing, but with the body, except the individual's physical good? What community of interest can there be except among spiritual beings, that reason, love, and hate on principles and under laws altogether distinct from any that regulate material combinations and results?

If degrees of criminality, as some men teach, be determined by the relative development of portions of our brains, and not according to the degree of our knowledge and the kind of motives presented to our reason, through our affections in our training, then the language of the Great Teacher is a violence to our nature,—"*If I had not come and spoken unto them, they had not had sin: but now they have no cloke for their sin.*" These words appear to have no meaning, unless they signify that the extent of man's accountableness is commensurate with the degree of hóly truth applied to his understanding.

Although some of the prominent advocates of phrenology undoubtedly regard that somewhat rickety science as affording irresistible arguments in favour of the material theory of mind, and hence infer that the soul perishes with the body; yet there are many more who, most heartily following their confident leaders, believe themselves persuaded that phrenology is only a little less certain than the gospel; and who nevertheless would not for the world forego their convictions of a spi-

ritual and immortal existence.   Some have taken
a kind of middle ground, and while staunch in
their attachment to the Christian creed, yet ima-
gining they possess proof in phrenological facts
that the soul has no being without the body, they
have endeavoured to prove to their own satisfaction that the Bible reveals not a word concerning
the distinct existence of the human spirit, but
rather that it declares an utter death of both soul
and body as derived from Adam.   But then they
dare not deny that an eternal life and bodily resurrection are promised and secured in Christ;
so they are brought to the conclusion, that when
a man dies he is annihilated as an individual
being, and by the power of God is reproduced on
some future occasion.   Dr. Elliotson, President
of the Phrenological Society, thus states, in the
Lancet, the position which he adopts : " By nature
all die, are utterly extinguished ; and in another
order of things, when the fashion of this world
shall have passed away and time shall be no more,
then in Christ, by the additional gift of God
granted through the obedience of Christ, but consequently by a miracle, not by our nature, we
shall all again be made alive." If Christianity be
true, then science, that is, the classification of natural facts, will never contradict it ; for God must
be the author of both.   The scientific part of
phrenology is therefore perfectly compatible with

revelation.   But infidelity has deeply stained the speculative and baseless assumptions which hasty reasoners have attached to that as well as other inquiries.   It is however delightful to find that men of the profoundest science most reverentially acknowledge that man and Christianity are productions of the same mind, and that there is nothing in any science at variance with the New Testament.   Yet I cannot help thinking that Dr. Elliotson, whom we must believe to be a sincere Christian, on his own confession of hope for eternal life through Jesus Christ, has followed a false interpretation in the passage above quoted; for how is it to be reconciled with these texts?—— *" Whosoever liveth and believeth in me shall never die." " This day shalt thou be with me in paradise." " We are confident and willing to be absent from the body and to be present with the Lord." " For we know that if our earthly house of this tabernacle were dissolved, we have a house not made with hands, eternal in the heavens."* These sentences seem plainly to express the fact of a spiritual existence, or being, at present distinct from the body, and capable of existence at once in another sphere. An array of arguments is not needed ——this is sufficient; unless such language, and the abundance of the same kind in the New Testament, can be proved to mean the reverse of the apparent meaning.

According to the newest fashion of phrenology, it is asserted that intellect and emotion, which imply will, operate through the brain as developed in the front of the head; and that will, associated with intellect, emotion, and instinctive propensity, acts upon the little brain behind, and part of the spinal chord, so as to excite muscular motion and expression.   These conclusions may perhaps have been demonstrated, yet all we can infer from such presumed facts is, that the instruments or organs merely constitute the media of communication between the world without and the world within, the material creation and the spiritual.   Facts are really best explained by supposing a unity of all the senses with the brain, and that the spirit, or perceptive and willing power, has faculties superadded, which are in correspondence with different portions of the brain, and therefore capable of being acted upon by it and acting with it.   But how do some phrenologists account for the operation of compound motives, such as we often feel?   They say it is done by a sort of sub-committee of the organs—by a board of control.   As Abernethy used to say, " Pho, pho, if they go to a board of control, I am content."   They thereby at once declare the necessity of a presiding and individual intelligence, endowed with various faculties as the properties of one being, subject to pain or pleasure, repugnance or desire, according as the objects presented to the mind through the senses are adapted, or otherwise, to these faculties or endowments, which are all associated with the will, in as far as they are all connected with a sense of the agreeable or disagreeable; and their very exercise consists in seeking the one and avoiding the other.

Perceiving, thinking, willing. Meditate on these things. What are they? Look upon the brain and think. Now put the idea of a brain and your experience of thought and feeling together; then say whether organization perceives, reflects, determines. Is thinking a property of the brain? No: the brain possesses all its material properties as well when dead as when living, and is as much a brain when uninfluenced by thought as when by it excited; therefore thinking is not a property of the brain: for if the properties of a substance be destroyed, the substance itself is destroyed. Is the brain constituted to secrete thought and feeling, as some assert? Where is the analogy between it and other secerning organs? Doubtless it may, and most likely does, separate something from the blood, perhaps electricity; and this it may do, because electricity is evolved in the circulation. All other secerning organs obtain and secrete matter chemically like that existing in the blood; but philosophers have not yet invented tests delicate enough to detect the elements of thought in the blood, where of course they ought to be, if separable from it by the brain.   But this is a vulgar view of materialism.   The philosophic materialists are more profound and refined. Doubtless with honest purpose they push on science to its limits; and finding matter everywhere, and spirit nowhere, they conclude that their own intellect results from atomic affinities, and of course that the mind of the universe—God, if He be—springs from eternal matter, which of course had no maker.   In short, matter is their visible almighty, and physical laws are his attributes and perfections.   No wonder then that they believe in eternal death; the wonder is that they live and feel and thus reason.

Surely as life is something more than mechanism, so thought is something above both.   No mixture of substances can produce life, much less mind. Every living thing is something more than matter, something more distinct from matter than the elements are from each other; and it has been propagated, imparted, and extended from a preceding life, in a manner which matter cannot be; after a type existing in egg or seed, at first impregnated by the spirit of life, and hence evolving itself in onward generations, still multiplying while advancing.   Thus also is it with the mind, which is something more than life; and every hu-

man spirit is like an imperishable reflection and
visible evidence of Eternal Being, which first fell
upon matter when Jehovah breathed life into
man's body, and saw in man's mental and moral
existence the everlasting image of Himself.

CHAPTER VII.

THE NATURE OF THE NERVOUS SYSTEM AND ITS OBEDIENCE TO THE WILL.

THE nervous system is, perhaps, merely a galvanic apparatus; so contrived as that by it the chemistry of life is carried on, and those states of the organs produced, which best enable the mind to receive sensation and to act on the body. That nerves, under the action of will, are capable of eliciting electricity, is proved by its actual production in the torpedo, the electric eel, and other creatures that possess an arrangement of nerves and muscles by which they can, at will, until fatigued, accumulate and discharge a succession of shocks. Indeed a spark from the electric eel may be made visible and conducted in a circle as from an ordinary electrical machine. The creature has a perfect galvanic apparatus extending from one end of its body to the other, supplied by two hundred and twenty-four pairs of nerves, which have no other office but to energize this apparatus, thus affording the most positive proof that the nervous power is essential to its galvanic action. Here then we find a living body capable of fulfilling all the purposes of a powerful voltaic pile, while its action or its quiescence is determined by another still more mysterious agency, namely, the will of the animal. And here also we again obtain a conclusive evidence that will is the act of a distinct agent, proving its distinctness by its control over a separate power.

"Weinhold, a German, cut off a cat's head, and when its arterial pulsation had ceased, took out the spinal marrow and placed in its stead an amalgam of mercury, silver and zinc: immediately after this was done the pulsation recommenced, and the body made a variety of movements. He took away the brain and spinal marrow of another cat and filled the skull and vertebral canal with the same metallic mixture. Life appeared to be instantly restored; the animal lifted up its head, opened and shut its eyes and looking with fixed stare, *endeavoured* to walk; and whenever it dropped, *tried* to raise itself on its legs. It continued in this state twenty minutes, when it fell down and remained motionless. During all the time the animal was thus treated, the circulation of the blood appeared to go on regularly; the secretion of gastric juice was more than usual, and the animal heat was established." *Lancet*, Sept. 2nd, 1843.

If it be true that the cat really tried to walk, and there seems no reason to doubt the experiment, it proves that the power which wills

E

and feels resides not in the brain and spinal chord, for it continued capable of acting after these were removed: therefore the brain is not necessary to its existence; and other galvanic media act also as stimuli to the organs through which volition evinces itself.

It has long been well known that galvanism, or electricity, for they are but modifications of the same thing, is capable of exciting motion even in the dead body, when transmitted through a muscle or a nerve of volition. We see that the will in the torpedo and electric eel produces both electricity and motion, and we find that a lifeless limb may be moved by electricity without the will; what can be a more natural hypothesis therefore than that electricity is excited through the nervous mass by the operation of the will, so as to produce muscular action? The exhaustion of the torpedo's power of exercising the will, in giving a shock, is an example of what always takes place when the will has been long or powerfully exerted. The nervous apparatus ceases to supply that electric power which stimulates the muscle; so that it may be used by the will, and the creature lies tired and torpid till restored by rest.

Thus we obtain a plausible theory of weariness or weakness: the nervous system becomes unfit to provide the proper stimulus to the muscular fibre. Rest is necessary to accumulate the electricity which must be produced from the sanguineous circulation. This state of exhaustion may be induced quite as readily by thinking as by bodily exertion, for the nervous system is as much excited by the one as by the other. Indeed, that the former, when intense, is more injurious to the bodily functions than the latter, and is not so easily repaired by rest and nourishment, will be shown as we proceed.

Thinking, with the use of the senses or with an effort of the will in maintaining attention, is so far a bodily action or function, and that of the most exhausting kind, but the more so because not accompanied by a corresponding force of circulation and of breathing, as in active employment of the limbs. It is remarkable that insane persons, whose course of thought, even when most excited, is unattended by voluntary mental effort, are not nearly so soon exhausted as studious persons, who think consecutively and with the attention fixed on their subject by the mere force of their will.

The power of the determination sometimes acts beyond the strength of the body. A boxer aims a blow at his antagonist, he misses his object, and he breaks the bone of his own arm. The cause is merely that the mind's action on the muscle was more powerful than the bone could bear. This energy of mind in the muscles is sometimes wonderfully exhibited by a poor emaciated madman. The strong men cannot hold him; for though his muscles are mere threads, the violence of his will under phrenzy of the brain endows them with untiring action. But the power of the will upon the muscle is best seen in the fact, that the very fibres that during life might have been employed to lift a hundred weight, may instantly after death be torn by the weight of a few ounces. Thus we find that, even now, the mind acts by imparting a power superior to any within the range of mechanics, and which absolutely confers strength on the material in which it operates, by adding to the attraction of cohesion, and perhaps overcoming gravitation, as electricity converts the soft iron into a mighty magnet; yet there is no real similarity between these facts. Will energizing atoms has no analogy but in the direct operation of Deity on the universe, which he actuates and inhabits.

But let us observe what occurs when a man moves. Here is no preparation but that of the will; he walks because he wills to walk; his mind's act is immediately obeyed by his body. There is no knowledge of the instruments employed, no idea of nerves and fibres. The mind is sensibly in every limb, and acts whenever it pleases to act, provided the mechanism be fit for use.   It must be in contact with the instrument, for it cannot act without; it cannot act where it is not, therefore the body bounds the power of the mind.   There is no reason why it should not act indefinitely with a suitable organization, for even now its energy is limited only by the imperfection of the materials it employs; and in the present economy of our bodies we possess a type of what we need—an untiring machinery.   There exists such a distribution of nervous power to certain parts, as the heart and the muscles by which we perform the act of breathing, that they are incapable of being fatigued.

A structure completely adapted to the energies of the unshackled soul, must be one that would offer no impediment to motion, be incapable of exhaustion, or, like a perpetual lamp, fed with power as fast as it is used; be indestructible, invulnerable; in short, a vehicle, like that in the prophet's vision, so entirely governed by the resident spirit, as to be whithersoever the spirit would,—not in subjection to earthly attractions and common cohesion, but a glorious body, fit to be the everlasting associate of the immortal soul; such as the inspired apostle describes as springing from the grave at the word of God,—a celestial, a spiritual, an incorruptible body.   Why should we deem this impossible? Do we not now feel that *this*

flesh is no match for the mighty spirit? Do we
not mourn the wretchedness of being forced for
its sake to stop short in our pursuit of pleasure or
of knowledge? Do we not know that this poor
trembling tissue is too weak to bear the full force
of even our narrow will? Shall we wonder then
that the faithful and almighty Father should fully
accommodate his children, and determine, if we
rightly seek it, to furnish each one with a spiritual and an incorruptible body, that we may the
better accomplish his will and thus enjoy our being.

It must be acknowledged that the language
employed in revealing the doctrine of a resurrection of the body, certainly favors the notions of
materialists, so far as it implies that the use of a
body of some kind is essential to the full and perfect capacity of human existence; but still it
proves that the spirit is not derived from the flesh,
and that it is distinct from physical arrangement;
and so far from depending on the body, the body
is to be reconstructed with new laws and functions, not to produce the being—man, but to accommodate him suitably in some other sphere of
action.

Some men sneer at the doctrine of a bodily resurrection, and others regard it with undefined
reverence, while perhaps both are equally far from
believing all its fulness; that is, they do not view
the doctrine in all its relations and with all the

sublime connexions as expressly revealed and demonstrated by one crowning fact,—the miracle has
happened. Those who receive the doctrine loosely,
are in danger of losing sight of its grand importance, and, having no distinct perception of its necessity, just as revealed, for the completion of the
Christian scheme, they may at length confound the
speculative fancies of their own whimsical minds,
and the dreaming comments of others, with what
God has spoken and done, so as to render the whole
subject a ridiculous incongruity instead of a sublime and consistent truth.   The mixture of falsehood with fact, calm reason must reject; and the
reasoner too often does not discover that what he
has rejected is but a deformity, and not the doctrine of the New Testament.   Thus the key-stone
of the bridge over the vast dark gulf between
time and eternity is gone, and he finds no footing
when his spirit would travel off this earth.   But
let the man who, in any manner, discredits the
resurrection, turn away from metaphysical questions and look at Christ—living, dead, buried,
risen! Or if he have tenderly loved one departed
in the living faith of a risen Lord, let him again
realize the presence and fellowship of the beloved
object in the promise and the prophecy of death-
less love and eternal happiness.   Then let the
bright vision again fade away in death and gloom,
without a star-gleam on the lonely grave; and

when his spirit seems in outer darkness, let the mourner read the 15th chapter of the 1st of Corinthians, and then call the doctrine of the resurrection a trick and a delusion if he can.   But we must return from this divergence.

CHAPTER VIII.

THE POWER OF ATTENTION, AND ITS CONNEXION WITH SLEEP.

LET us again reflect a little on the power of attention. Is this a property of the body? Can the body produce a faculty capable of *regarding* its own wants and influencing its own sensations? If you cease to attend to the senses, you cease to be conscious of external existence; your body necessarily falls asleep, or you pass into a state of reverie. The body is not then needed for any of the voluntary acts of the mind. It is not then wanted by the will; and therefore until some interference with the repose of the body happens, or some power agitates its resident spirit, and thus demands the use of the organization subservient to the will, you continue without attention to external objects. We have no proof, however, that the soul also slumbers; but we have reason rather to conclude that it attends to the past when not engaged with things present. At least we know we often dream, and to dream is the business of the mind when combining past impressions, with-

out regard to the actual state of the body. When
we awake we generally forget our dreams, because
the soul again wills and acts in keeping with circumstances around us; and the machinery of the
body, if in health, again obeys the mandates of
the mind. There is something operating which
is so unlike all it influences, that it can neither
be seen, nor handled, nor at all perceived, but in
its action upon matter.

When not using the body, that is, when not
employing material substances, the mind acknowledges neither time nor space, for it is not governed by physical laws. Hence it is that, if
no haunting anxiety perplex the mind and no
disorder disturb the organism of the associate
body, as often, and as regularly as the curtain of
nightly shade falls around us, and we desire to
withdraw our attention, the senses sleep; and,
at the touch of light, the consenting spirit within
again awakes them to the wonders of a daily
resurrection. During the interval between the
evening and morning, what intricate visions of
activity and interest, all according to some law
important to our being, crowd upon the busy
soul, not indeed in the distinctness of a measured
and material succession, but as if at once past
and yet present. There is no consciousness of
time in our dreams; for a sense of time arises
from a comparison of the relative duration of

material changes, and therefore belongs only to the outward use of the mind. In the imaginings or fanciful but instructive blendings of past ideas in our profounder slumbers, we are but in the spirit, without the perception of circumstances; and the action of the soul, like itself, has no dependance on minutes and hours; for it knows no division, no dimensions, and is comprehended only by the mind of Him who produced it. But even in sleep the spirit usually preserves a kind of discriminating vigilance with regard to the sense of hearing at least, so as to distinguish the meaning of sounds. Thus the mother, whose mind is naturally engrossed by the infant that depends on her for every help, will sleep profoundly amidst the incessant din and rattle of a London thoroughfare, or of carriages and the rout, it may be next door, but the smallest sound from her baby will instantly awaken her.

This perception during sleep, however, must be greatly modified by the previous habit and by the state of mind at the time. One unaccustomed to the rushing and roaring of a steam-vessel at sea would scarcely be able to sleep, but the captain would probably start up in a moment if the engine were to stop.

The action of the mind on the circulation, and the development of nervous energy in the use of the senses and muscles, while we are awake, is of

so positive and exhausting a nature, as regards
the powers of the body, that a continuance of
sleeplessness must terminate in death.   There is
reason to believe that growth or addition to the
body never takes place while the senses are engaged, in consequence of the demand made by
the mind in maintaining their action.   What we
understand by fatigue is the felt unfitness of the
body any longer to subserve the outward purposes
of the mind.   If we do not yield to the sense of
weariness, but struggle against it by strong effort;
or if, in consequence of some interesting subject
engrossing the affections and powerfully exciting
the will, we find that we cannot sleep, the body
rapidly becomes diseased, and the manifestations
of the mind assume an irregular and disordered
character.   In short, long-continued vigilance is
a frequent cause of insanity as well as of other
bodily maladies.   It is remarkable, however, that
when mental derangement is established from this
cause, the patient often regains a considerable
degree of bodily vigour, although he enjoy an
extremely small degree of perfect sleep.   This
fact is probably explained by the circumstance
that the insane person does not use his senses in
the same attentive manner as a sane individual,
but he behaves as if acting in a dream.   The
brain in such cases is but partially awake, or at
least is in such a state that the mind cannot so

act upon it as to keep it in the condition necessary for orderly and vigilant thinking; and therefore it cannot be exhausted as we experience it to be by mental effort. The madman's thoughts, like dreams, are fashioned into fantastic and mysterious visions, in keeping indeed with his past history and remembrance; the ideas are impressed upon his living soul, but irrespective of any resolute demand of his will, though never as I believe without relation to his moral characteristics.

Sleep results from a constitutional bodily necessity; the attention of the mind must be withdrawn from the body, or the machinery of nerves and blood-vessels cannot be properly repaired and fitted for further action. The body requires rest, the mind does not; and the body needs it only because the structure of its parts will not bear the incessant operation of the mind upon it. Unless the structure be rendered quite unfit for the use of the mind, it is always roused into action whenever an appeal is made to the soul by any influence. In short, it is manifest that the thinking and acting principle does not sleep at all in the sense in which the body sleeps when the mind is not using it; for the mind is always ready for action whenever the organization is in a fit state to convey impression and to be employed. As surely as physical phenomena excite sensation during sleep, as in some dreams, so surely do they prove that during sleep there is no absolute suspension of the faculty of perception. That we awake at the bidding of a bodily necessity, as also we fall asleep, is an evidence that the mind only partially retires from the senses till outward occasion demands the physical operation of the will.

It is simply ridiculous to say, as some do, that the brain is *actively employed* in taking up recollected impressions of the thousand associations of past thought and feeling in dreaming and insanity, and yet to deny that the brain produces mind; for if the mind does not recollect these past associations, the brain must; but as manifested mind (so called) consists of these very thoughts and feelings, mind itself, as a distinct thing, has no existence, if their production and reproduction be only a function of the brain. The cessation of the brain is then the cessation of the thinking principle,—they are one. Is it not more reasonable to consider dreaming and insanity as mind or soul in action, without any distinctness of exterior purpose or aim, such as we feel while acting in our social relations and in consciousness of responsibility, because we then recognize the propriety of those laws by which our actions should be governed in relation to others and for our own sakes?

Ideas are remembered impressions, and dreams

are confused ideas; if then ideas are mental, dreams are mental. There are laws under which the soul acts in dreaming as well as in thinking, and it is often difficult to distinguish these acts. Neither the danger nor the absurdity of considering dreaming as a mental act is very apparent, notwithstanding this opinion has been regarded with a sort of pious dread by some writers, who attribute dreaming to the spontaneous action of an irritated brain; as if they escaped from the dilemma of materialism by representing waking ideas as the result of a spiritual intelligence, and those arising during sleep as the sole offspring of a writhing bundle of fibres. Such timid reasoning, after all its agony, only pictures the mind as more completely an accident of matter, unless such language be meant merely to signify that ideas in sleep are not directed by the same degree or kind of mental determination as during the periods of vigilance and wilfulness. This, however, no one denies; and it is perfectly consistent with the notion that the being that thinks is stimulated by impressions derived through the nervous system,—it is actuated by motive, by the agreeable or disagreeable; but then the nervous system, which only communicates the causes of sensations, not the sensations themselves, cannot originate the thinking being itself, nor confer any of its properties. It is the property of this being to be roused into ordinary activity by impressions on the nerves; and all the phenomena of dreams and disorder of the brain are precisely such as we should look for under such an arrangement, when we reflect that the attention is more or less withdrawn from the senses in these cases, as we shall discover by reference to facts.

Experiment demonstrates that the power of attending to the senses may be influenced by the occupation of the mind or by the state of the organization, and of course our common consciousness or unconsciousness, when we are not asleep, is only the condition of the soul in regard to the senses, that is, to external attention. In dreaming there is always consciousness at the time of the ideas passing, and yet on waking we do not always, nor indeed generally, remember that we have dreamed; so that in fact we are conscious in one state without being aware of it in another. This fact is abundantly proved, as we shall see, and it furnishes demonstration that the mind may be active during what we call a state of insensibility, and may require only some slight change in the connexion of the faculty or power of soul by which we remember, to enable us to recall with distinctness the condition and employment of mind during such a state of apparent suspense; just as we recognize in waking

memory the various experiences of our wakeful
life. Some link in the chain is wanting to complete the circle, which, being completed, one end
is connected with the other; the current of
thought returns, and we become conscious of its
unbroken action. There is no possibility of understanding this subject, without bearing in mind
our double consciousness, that with the senses
and that without their use. But it is fruitless to
attempt reasoning without facts; these supersede
all other arguments, and to facts therefore we
shall always appeal. Yet we should not disregard
the suggestion that the mind may possess a power,
hereafter to be developed, by which it shall be
enabled to connect all its ideas and dreams together, and perceive the mutual relation of its two
states of consciousness.

CHAPTER IX.

THE STATE OF THE WILL IN DREAMING.

THINKING is that action of the mind by which we become conscious of existence, either in the remembrance of the past, the perception of the present, or the expectation of the future. Thought, as it regards our observation of facts, is always voluntary. An act of the will precedes or accompanies attention, whether to sensible or ideal objects. As our experience is actual, we of course at once associate sensation with an object; hence imagination, or the action of mind abstract from sense, supplies an appropriate succession of ideas, by the law of association. The faculty of conceiving unreal circumstances, or things not present, although ordinarily unattended by volition in the restricted sense, yet never proceeds altogether without the operation of the will; for mental abstraction commences and is maintained by a determinate effort. In this case, however, we preserve a certain control over the body. But in dreams, or in reverie of the most profound kind, the mind seems more detached from the physical organization. Still even then we attend to the ideas presented, and, to a great extent, reason and decide concerning them according to the moral principles which habitually regulate our conduct; so that in fact our dreams would well reveal to us the state of our hearts and our habits, for in them our wills are freer from restraint, and our desires are more undisguised by the hypocrisies of waking life. As Sir Thomas Browne says in his tract on dreams, "Persons of radical integrity will not easily be perverted in their dreams, nor noble minds do pitiful things in sleep." "Though bounded in a nut-shell, I might fancy myself a king of infinite space, but that I have had dreams," exclaims Hamlet. These visions of the night indeed instruct us concerning our characters; and though they are produced involuntarily, yet they test the conscience and prove the state of our dispositions. The facts about to be related will fully confirm the truth of this observation, and assist to sustain the opinion that all thinking is influenced by the previous habit and training of the will.

That volition is not suspended during sleep, is proved by many facts; and probably the experience of every person who remembers his dreams, affords evidence that the will is as busy during sleep as when awake. But the fact is strikingly illustrated by examples of remarkable exertion of will, in the employment of intellect and genius during sleep. Tartini, a celebrated violin player, composed his famous *Devil's Sonata* while he dreamed that the devil challenged him to a trial of skill on his own violin. Cabanis often during his dreams saw clearly into the bearing of political events which baffled him when awake. Condorcet frequently left his deep and complicated calculations unfinished when obliged to retire to rest, and found their results unfolded in his dreams. Coleridge's account of his wild composition, *Kubla Khan,* is very curious. He had been reading *Purchas's Pilgrimage,* and fell asleep at the moment he was reading this sentence—" Here the Khan Kubla commanded a palace to be built, and a stately garden thereunto." He continued in profound sleep about three hours, during which he had a vivid confidence that he composed from two to three hundred lines; if, as he says, that can be called composition in which all the images rose up before him as *things* with a parallel production of correspondent expressions. On awaking he appeared to have a distinct recollection of the whole, and proceeded to write down the wonderful lines that are preserved, when he was interrupted, and could never afterwards recall the rest.

We might multiply examples, but all we could adduce would demonstrate no more than the fore-

going, though they might afford additional presumption that the mind is generally employed
during sleep, on its chosen or accustomed subjects, and that dreams indicate our spiritual condition, because in them those faculties and feelings
are most active which we most energetically exercise while awake.

In short, it appears that the contact of any
disturbing power with the mind, whether awake
or asleep, necessarily causes it to act and will
according to its habit and character. Every new
sensation is unaccountably connected with some
preceding sensation, so that volition and memory
are the necessary characteristics of manifested
mind. No subtilty of reasoning has been able to
account for these powers or peculiarities of mind
on a material theory. Phrenologists and meta-
physicians, with all their grand and cloudy pre-
tensions, have added nothing important to our
knowledge concerning them. All their elaborate
disquisitions exhibiting the operation of mental
function in unison with organization, teach us no
more than we previously knew, namely, that the
functions of the mind and brain are created to
act together at present. They leave us in possession of the capital and most interesting fact,
that *we do will* and *we do remember*, but they
cannot tell us how. Still they must acknowledge
that these wonderful powers result from the ope-

ration of some thing or being, which *chooses* between pleasant and unpleasant sensations, both *when the body sleeps and when it wakes*; and which some thing or being also recalls past impressions according to certain laws of association and certain states of mind and body. That is, our Maker has bound our faculties to act in a certain order, under certain circumstances; in short, that He holds dominion over mind as well as matter, for purposes hereafter to be revealed.

CHAPTER X.

ILLUSTRATIONS OF THE POWER OF THE MIND IN DREAMING, SOMNAMBULISM, &c.

THE importance of reflecting on volition and memory will be best demonstrated by facts, and an acquaintance with these principles will most fully manifest the nature of our existence, as constituted to be modified and actuated by moral forces. The senses are impressed whenever their objects are present, but the mind itself receives no impression unless disposed to attend. Thus we find that when the mind is fully intent upon one class of objects or ideas, it wholly disregards all others; as when the absent man forgets the presence of his friends, or the imaginative man revels in his ideal world to the detriment of his well-being in this lower and more palpable existence. Many curious instances of this want of attention to the senses may be related, the most remarkable of which very nearly approximate to insanity, which probably in most cases is properly described as being out of the senses. Those images and intimations which the senses continue correctly to exhibit, are disregarded or perverted by the mind while it is busied about sensations or impressions produced or excited by some disordered action of the brain; which being the organ on which the thinking power immediately acts, and through which it directly receives all its intelligence concerning the external world, of course must constantly modify the manifestation of mind according to the healthiness of its structure and function. Somnambulism, or sleep-walking, affords good examples of mental activity without attention to the impression made on the senses. Somnambulists generally walk with their eyes open, but it is evident that they do not employ them. A man has been known to fall asleep while walking at the end of a fatiguing journey, and he could not be roused from his sleep without great difficulty, although he continued to walk in company with his friends for a considerable distance. It is indeed a well-authenticated fact, that in the disastrous retreat of Sir John Moore, many of the soldiers fell asleep, yet continued to march along with their comrades.

In connexion with this subject we have an illustration of the genius of Shakspeare. He was so observant of nature and so well distinguished the apparent from the actual, that his descriptions even of disease are so marvellously truthful that the teacher of pathology may often quote them as the best guides to his pupils. He gives a lucid glimpse at the phenomena of somnambulism and sleep-talking, when he describes Lady Macbeth in "the unnatural troubles of her unnatural deeds, discharging the secrets of her infected mind to her deaf pillow." He represents the abrupt and suggestive vision of circumstances, in which the soul re-enacts her terrible part, precisely as those often witness who are attendant on talking dreamers and insane persons. The only evident difference between these classes is, that the latter seem to dream on when quite awake, and force their senses to confirm their fancies.

"I have seen her rise from her bed," says the gentlewoman, "throw her night-gown upon her, unlock her closet, take forth paper, fold it, write upon it, read it, afterwards seal it, and again return to bed; yet all this while fast asleep."

> " *Doct.*—You see her eyes are open.
> *Gent.*—But their sense is shut."

In these cases we observe that the mind controls the actions of the voluntary muscles, and continues attending to visible objects, without employing the sense of sight, and apparently receives impressions of sound, while the auditory nervous apparatus is quite insensible. It may be true that certain portions of brain sleep while other portions remain awake; but what does that

F

signify? Can one part of the brain subserve the purposes of the other parts, and those organs which phrenologists appropriate to thought, furnish a substitute in their own action for that of the instruments of vision and of hearing? If so, their system must be false; for faculty is not limited according to their cranial maps, the provinces of which are boldly defined by very imaginary lines indeed. But what is the difference in the state of the brain during sleeping and waking? Happily we are supplied with facts which in some measure answer this question, and prove to our satisfaction that both brain and mind act altogether, and not by bits.

Sir Astley Cooper had a patient, whose skull being imperfect allowed him to examine the movements of the brain. Sir Astley says, " I distinctly saw the pulsation of the brain was regular and and slow, but at this time he was *agitated by some opposition to his wishes,* and directly the blood was sent with increased force to the brain, the pulsation became frequent and violent." Dr. Pierquin witnessed the following case in the hospital of Montpellier, in 1821. Dr. Caldwell states that " the subject of it was a female, who had lost a large portion of the skull and *dura mater* in a neglected attack of *lues venerea.* When she was in a dreamless sleep her brain was motionless; when her sleep was imperfect and she was agitated by dreams, her brain protruded from the cranium; in vivid dreams, *reported as such by herself*, the protrusion was considerable; and when perfectly awake, especially if engaged in active thought or sprightly conversation, it was greater still." We may observe that in dreams reported by herself to be vivid, the brain protruded. These dreams must then have occurred during the transition from sleep to waking, for we shall learn from numerous other facts that the most perfect dreams are those which are not remembered. Here, moreover, we have a demonstration that the brain is roused by the mind; for mind must first have responded to the call, whatever the medium of the sensation which caused the patient to awake. We also see that the brain, during active thought, must have been injected with additional blood in every part of it, for doubtless it would have become enlarged in all directions at once, had the skull allowed. This must always be the tendency whenever the supply of blood is increased in the brain, if we understand anything of its mechanism and circulation; for branches spread to every part from the larger blood vessels; and as there are no valves the supply must flow to all, as water flows through every open pipe connected with the main. But perhaps some questioner would suggest that the mind possesses power to control the supply, and cause it to pass with more or less freedom in certain parts of the brain, according to circumstances. This indeed may readily be granted; for it substantiates what is contended for, namely, that the mind acts independently and as a whole, not as a loose bundle of separate faculties, each self-moved; and that mind acts according to its will, that is its nature, taking this or that direction as it is impressed.

Yet we have no proof that brain thus responds in parcels to the impress of the mind, and even if we had, it would no more prove that mind results from the action of the brain than from the use of our limbs, through which also the mind is manifested by calling them into action. At any rate, the oneness of the mind, and therefore its independence on successive conditions of brain and faculty, must be acknowledged; for surely it is the same mind which experiences all the successions of sensation and of thought. How then does this fact agree with the assumption that the healthy brain may be active in one part and dormant in another? The state and power of attention alone explain the mystery. We find that mental activity, when directed to the body, causes an instantaneous increase in the supply of blood to the brain, which of course we should expect, because the blood furnishes the material, whether electrical or not, which excites the whole bodily apparatus into action when the will demands it.

This fact, however, brings us very little nearer to the unravelment of the tangled clue that must guide us from the mazes of science and surmise.

It is evident that the integrity of mental action is not dependant on the waking activity of the brain, or at least of that portion of it which is more immediately connected with the senses; for, notwithstanding the last-mentioned facts, we possess incontrovertible evidence in preceding facts that the mind is sometimes employed more clearly in profound sleep than when the attention is in any degree directed to the senses. Dr. Abercrombie relates, that an eminent lawyer had been consulted respecting a case of great difficulty and importance, and after several days of intense attention to the subject, he got up in his sleep and wrote a long paper. The following morning he told his wife that he had had a most interesting dream, and that he would give anything to recover the train of thought which had then passed through his mind. She directed him to his writing desk, where he found his opinion clearly and luminously written out.

It is contrary to all the physiology of the case to conclude, as some most hastily have done, that it is but a lighter kind of sleep which is associated with somnambulism; for this condition results from nervous exhaustion, and is apt, like delirium, to occur in the most marked manner in persons

in whom the quantity of blood is deficient. The
difficulty of arousing such patients is always in
proportion to the completeness of the attack ; that
is, in proportion to the energy with which the
will is at work without attending to the body,—a
sufficient proof that the sleep, whether partial or
perfect, is yet profound. This kind of sleep never
seems to happen but when the nervous system
demands unusual repose, being greatly worn by
some bodily irritation or mental disquietude. The
abuse of the passions most frequently predisposes
to its worst forms. That the mind should act
thus vigorously when the body is exhausted, and
be most energetic when the heart beats low and
the cheek is blanched, is at best but indifferent
attestation to the truth of the theory that requires
mind to be merely the effect of blood acting upon
brain, or a kind of compound engendered by their
mixture, which will be most strongly manifested
when the mixture is most active, like the electric
fluid from the acid and the metals in the galvanic
trough.

Dr. Darwin *(Zoonomia,* p. 221), relates a case
which he witnessed, of a young lady who, after
being exhausted by violent convulsions, was suddenly affected by what he calls reverie. She conversed aloud with imaginary persons, her eyes
were open, but so intently was her mind occupied
that she could not be brought to attend to exter-

nal objects by the most violent stimulants. The conversations were quite consistent. Sometimes she was angry, at other times very witty, but most frequently inclined to melancholy. Indeed it appears that this reverie only exalted her natural versatility of temper and intellect. She sang with accuracy, and repeated many pages from the poets. In repeating some lines from Pope, she forgot a word, and after repeated trials regained it. In subsequent attacks she could walk about the room, and, although she could not see, she never ran against the furniture, but always avoided obstacles. Dr. Darwin convinced himself that in this state she was *not capable of seeing or hearing* in the ordinary manner. It is observable in this case that volition was not suspended; she regained by effort the lost word in repeating the poetry, and deliberated according to the natural habit of her mind; yet, when the paroxysm was over, she could not recollect a single idea of what had passed in it.

The relation between dreaming and somnambulism is remarkably exhibited by the manner in which the current of dreams may be directed in certain individuals, by impressing their senses during sleep. An officer, engaged in the expedition to Louisburg, in 1758, was so peculiarly susceptible of such impressions that he afforded his companions much amusement by the facility with which they could cause him to dream. Once they conducted him through a quarrel which ended in a duel: the pistol was placed in his hand, he fired, and was awakened by the report. They found him asleep on a locker, when they made him believe he had fallen overboard. They told him a shark was pursuing him, and entreated him to dive for his life, and he threw himself with great force on the cabin floor. After the landing of the army at Louisburg, his friends found him one day asleep in his tent, and evidently much annoyed by the cannonading. They then made him believe he was engaged, when he expressed great fear and a disposition to run away. They remonstrated, but increased his fears by imitating groans, and when he asked who was hit, they named his particular friends. At last they told him the man next him had fallen, when he sprang out of bed, rushed out of the tent, and ended his dream by falling over the tent ropes. He had no recollection of his dreams.

The following instance is related in the first volume of the *Lancet*. George Davies, 16 years old, in the service of Mr. Hewson, Butcher, of Bridge-road, Lambeth, being fatigued, bent forward in his chair, and, resting his forehead on his hands, fell asleep. After ten minutes he started up, went for his whip, put on his spurs, and went to the stable. Not finding his own saddle in the

proper place, he returned to the house and asked
for it. Being asked what he wanted with it, he
replied to go his rounds. He returned to the
stable, got on the horse without the saddle, and
was proceeding to the street, when, with much
difficulty and force, he was removed from his
horse. He thought himself stopped at the turn-
pike gate, took sixpence out of his pocket to be
changed, and holding out his hand for the change,
the sixpence was returned to him. He immediately observed, "None of your nonsense; that is
the sixpence again,—give me my change." When
2½d. was given to him, he counted it over and
said, "None of your gammon—that is not right
—I want a penny more;" making the 3½d., which
was his proper change. He then said, "Give me
my *castor*" (meaning his hat), which slang term
he had been in the habit of using, and then began to whip and spur to get his horse on. Mr.
Hewson related the circumstance, in his hearing,
of a Mr. Harris, Optician, in Holborn, whose son,
some years since, walked out on the parapet of
the house in his sleep. The boy joined the conversation, and observed that he lived at the corner
of Brownlow-street. After being bled, he awoke,
got up, and asked what was the matter (having
then been one hour in the trance), not having
the slightest recollection of anything that had

passed. His eyes remained closed the whole of the time.

According to a report made by the Committee of the Royal Academy of Sciences at Paris, that process which is called Animal Magnetism appears to have the power of producing a remarkable kind of somnambulism. The facts about to be related seem too startling to be easily credited, but the testimony of such men as Cloquet, Georget, and Itard, is not to be lightly esteemed; and they all concur in bearing witness to the truth of the case. —A lady, 64 years of age, had a cancer in her breast. She was magnetized, as it is called, for the purpose of dissolving the tumor, but the only effect was to throw her into a state in which external sensibility was removed, while her ideas and power of conversing retained all their clearness. In this condition her surgeon induced her to submit to an operation. Having given her consent, she sat down on a chair, and the diseased part was deliberately dissected out, while she continued conversing about the different stages of the operation—being perfectly insensible of pain. On awaking, she had no consciousness whatever of having been operated upon. She was a lady of great respectability, and resided at No. 151, Rue St. Denis, Paris.

This case is not quoted either for or against

Mesmerism. The operation having been really performed, and the patient having appeared indifferent to pain, it equally well answers the purpose of illustration; for if truly the effect of mesmerism, it proves the power of causing a wonderful sort of abstraction, during which the mind may perceive what goes on in the organs, and employ them too, without sensation in them. And if this case be an imposition in that respect, it yet proves the mastery of the will in maintaining the attention according to purpose in almost as marvellous a manner. An anonymous opposer of Mesmerism lately announced, in a periodical, that the lady had confessed her imposition; but, on subsequent inquiry of the celebrated surgeon who operated, and of others who intimately knew her, they positively denied that there was any deception, or that she had ever confessed anything to that effect. When Dr. Caldwell, of America, asked M. Cloquet, who operated in this case, if he had ever seen a patient in the ordinary state who bore pain as unmoved, he answered, *"Jamais! jamais! jamais!"* He also said he was *quite sure that she never made the confession alluded to*. This subject will again claim our attention, when more fully and particularly considering the morbid influences of the mind on the body.

CHAPTER XI.

THE STATE OF THE ATTENTION MODIFIES SENSATION.

WE have reason to believe that whenever disordered action of the mind occurs, a corresponding disorder takes place in the nervous organization ; but it always manifests itself at first, and indeed more or less throughout its course, by new and irregular whimsicalities of will, the attention being withdrawn from ordinary objects, and the mind impressed by some false conviction or unreasonable desire. In short, insanity appears to be a disease in which the mind is rendered incapable of due attention, either to ideas existing in the memory or to new impressions on the senses, in consequence of being possessed by some false notion, to such an extent that it cannot view any subject or idea bearing any relation to that notion except in such a manner as shall confirm the false impression. Whatever is presented to the mind in association with that false impression, at once causes the mind, according to a common law of its operation, to attend to the prominent notion, which thus assumes the character of an indisput-

able truth—an axiom—a faith to which everything must conform. The following anecdote will
illustrate the power of this kind of false belief,
and at the same time demonstrate that mental
persuasion is superior to the impressions of bodily
necessity. A man will starve to death rather than
renounce what he regards as truth.

A clergyman, about 40 years of age, while
drinking wine, happened to swallow with it the
seal of a letter which he had just received. One
of his companions seeing him alarmed, for the
sake of a foolish jest, cried out, " It will seal up
your bowels." These words taking effect upon
his brain while excited by a fright, caused the
gentleman to become suddenly insane. From that
moment he was the victim of melancholy, and in
a few days he refused to swallow any kind of
nourishment, alleging as a reason that " he knew
nothing would pass through him." The plentiful
operation of a powerful cathartic, which his physician forced him to take, failed to convince him
of the patency of his bowels. Coaxing and threats
were equally unavailing; his mind would not
consent that anything should pass down into his
stomach, and he died of a mad idea.

All prejudice which disqualifies an individual
from comparing evidence is so far disorder of intellect. The will is thus engaged and cannot attend to new claimants, so as to determine justly

concerning them. In madness, the prejudice and perversion are more decided, and for the most part more honest than those which cause divisions amongst responsible men. Like children looking through different coloured glasses at the sun, each believes that his own fragment presents the only proper hue.

In mental derangement, the deficiency, as respects the power of attending to sensation, may be very partial and even limited to one subject. As regards that subject, the faculty of discrimination is lost. Any attempt to compare only reproduces the same image. Thus a man may believe, as the celebrated Simon Browne did, that he has lost his rational soul, while at the same time exerting the highest order of intellect. This person, in dedicating a controversial work to Queen Anne, says of himself, "he was once a man of some little name, but of no worth, as his present unparalleled case makes too manifest; for by the immediate hand of God, his very thinking substance has been wasting away for seventeen years till it is wholly perished." So completely does the dominant idea sometimes possess the attention, that certain deranged persons become almost insensible to external impressions, and are able, if they will, like that pseudo-saint, Macarius, to stand in a state of nudity for months together, in a marsh, exposed to the bite of every noxious insect.

The soul seems conscious only of those things that suit the state of its will. We see, whenever we have means of detecting it, that the will is always engaged about its business; for, as far as we can observe the mind's operations, it is ever comparing, choosing, or pursuing. We sleep, and lose sight of realities; we awake, and lose sight of dreams, only because our attention is fixed on what is present to the mind's consciousness of things external or within itself; but still, sleeping or waking, the thinking principle is equally intent and equally engaged. Circumstances change not its nature, but only modify its operation. Even apparent unconsciousness is no proof of its suspension. Let the same circumstances return, and the mind manifests itself in the same manner, for neither physical elements nor *spiritual dynamics* can alter the affinities of the soul or liberate it from the necessity of choice and action, according to the constitution in which it was created. The freedom of its will is limited to its sphere, and any contrariety in its movements to Divine Law brings it in contact with some obstacle, so that persistance in erroneous desire leads only to increased suffering; and as a creature is rendered incapable of its natural delight when in darkness, so every rational soul finds its proper liberty only in returning to the true light, which is true love.

Those forms of insanity, sleep-walking and

sleep-talking, which so frequently present themselves, prove, as before observed, that mental activity is not proportioned to the wakefulness of the senses, nor indeed necessarily associated with sensation, but rather the reverse; at least it appears that the mind in such cases is occupied not so much in attending to external things as to fancies; or if in any degree to realities, only so far as to mix them with imagined or remembered circumstances. This is perfectly consonant with all we know of the mind; for though ideas are first excited by some peculiar condition of the organization, in keeping with certain states of mental faculty, yet the ideas or images of things afterwards continue to play their parts in the dramas of the soul, without its recurring to the help of renewed sensation. The senses then are no part of our consciousness, or of ourselves, for individuality does not consist of parts; it is the one and indivisable being, the *ego ipse*, which perceives and wills.

The senses convey the exciting causes of new thoughts to our minds, but the elements of the thoughts themselves always reside in the mind, which forms the thought; for there is no necessary connexion between the sensation and the idea awakened by it but in the nature and property of the thinking principle itself. It is this which gives appropriate forms to appropriate impressions, or interprets sensations in keeping with some pre-existing ordinance of the soul. We see, we feel, we hear, according to a power apart from sense, or not necessarily associated with it, and according to a nature that may see, hear, feel, in a different manner with different instruments, or even immediately, that is, without instruments, and rather according to the state of the will than the state of the body.

Here an observation concerning the phenomena attributed to Mesmerism may be again ventured. If philosophical witnesses have not avouched fallacies and tricks to be facts and fair-dealing, we possess demonstration that sensation is not essential to perception; for men whom we have been accustomed to think shrewd physiologists, whose opinions in other matters have been deemed most wisely founded on observation, are ready to declare their conviction—that individuals in a certain state of mesmeric excitation, are in the habit of dispensing with the use of their senses in holding communication with things about them. The cases of clairvoyance are numerous, and related with all appearance of honest simplicity, in most of the treatises on Mesmerism. Now, if we may rely on these experiments, it follows,—

I. That the mind in the normal state perceives objects through sensation, but may, in a disturbed state, perceive objects directly.

II. Objects perceived directly convey the same impression with objects perceived through sensation; therefore external objects are real.

III. The mind is capable of acting independently of its organs; therefore the mind may exist without the body (*see Mayo on the Nervous System*). —Since then it is so boldly declared that facts from all quarters conduce to such important conclusions, it behoves the philosophic patiently to examine the records containing them, and, as far as possible, to test their truth by strict observation.

CHAPTER XII.

THE FACULTY OF ABSTRACTION.

THE preceding facts, being viewed in connexion, clearly prove that the mind is formed to be in action when impressed, and that it does not grow out of sensations, but is qualified to avail itself of their help in the acquisition of truth. In proportion as we become acquainted with moral relations, we become conscious of responsibility, and then our individuality takes its highest standing. We perceive that on the direction of our voluntary energies depends either our weal or our woe; because we possess the faculty of willing according to our knowledge, and of fixing our attention on objects according to the end we would attain. Let us not however venture upon the metaphysical quicksand, but turn to our common experience of that condition of the thinking principle in which we abstract our attention from surrounding objects, in order to fix it upon ideas existing in our memory or imagination.

The same being that employs a certain set of muscles for the accomplishment of its purposes, also exercises a control over the faculties with which his mind may be endowed, and to a great extent directs their operations according to the will, as long as the functions of the body allow. Probably in a perfect state, as regards physical accommodation, there would be no other limit to the exercise of this commanding power over the mental faculties than the necessary law of their constitution as mental, so that we might recall at will whatever passage of past experience we required to review, and, by the government of ideal associations, compare fact with fact as might best subserve the interests of our reason.

This power of reflecting on accumulated impressions in detail, appears to be the distinguishing characteristic of human intelligence. It is possessed by different individuals in very various degrees, and, like all our other endowments, may be vastly improved by proper employment. In some persons of acknowledged judgment, from inordinate exercise or from morbid indisposition, abstraction nevertheless becomes closely allied to insanity.

In the practice of abstraction, such as it is, the devotees of Budhism far excel our philosophers. It is indeed the highest attainment of that superstition for persons so far to abstract themselves, as to become unconscious of all external existence. Thus we find individuals among them habitually submitting with the most profound composure to inflictions and influences which, to ordinary mortals, would induce the most terrible torment; but they really do not feel them, because they determine not to feel.

The Fakirs invert their eyes in silent contemplation on the ceiling, then gradually looking down they fix both eyes, squinting at the tip of the nose, until, as they say, the blessings of a new light beam upon them. The Monks of Mount Athos were accustomed, in a manner equally ridiculous and with the same success, to hold converse, as they fancied, with the Deity. Allatius thus describes the directions for securing the celestial joys of Omphalopsychian contemplation :—— " Press thy beard upon thy breast, turn thine eyes and thoughts upon the middle of thine abdomen ; persevere for days and nights, and thou shalt know uninterrupted joys, when thy spirit shall have found out thy heart and illuminated itself." St. Augustin mentions a priest who could at will fall into these ecstacies, in which his senses were so forsaken by his soul as that he did not experience the pangs of the torture.

A modern astronomer passed a whole night in the same attitude, observing a phenomenon in the sky, and on being accosted by some of the family in the morning, he said, " It must be thus; I will go to bed before 'tis late !" He had gazed

the whole night and did not know it. The mathe-
matician, Viote, was sometimes so absorbed by
his calculations that he has been known to pass
three days and three nights without food. It is
related of the Italian poet, Marini, that while he
was intensely engaged in revising his Adonis, he
placed his leg on the fire where it burnt for some
time without his being aware of it. The power
of the mind in withdrawing itself from sensation
can scarcely be more strongly exemplified.

If a man of the finest faculties yields his reason
to the fascinations of sensuality, he soon loses
control over the associations of his mind; memory and judgment necessarily become impaired.
Even a brief interruption to the habit of mental
withdrawal from objects of sense, renders a return
to abstraction a greater effort, especially if the
senses have in the interval been occupied by objects that powerfully excite the passions. Hence
we see the necessity of comparative sequestration,
and temperate management of the body to the
student's success, and hence too we learn that
diversity of objects is the natural remedy for
morbid abstraction. The case of Brindley, the
celebrated engineer, illustrates these observations.
His memory and abstraction were so great, that
although he could scarcely read or write, he executed the most elaborate and complex plans as a
matter of course, without committing them to

paper. But this power was so completely disturbed after seeing a play, that he could not for a long time afterwards, resume his usual pursuits.

That degree of abstractedness which approaches to dreaming is so essential to powerful intellectual effort, that Dr. Macnish, in his "Philosophy of Sleep," includes all the higher exercises of genius in his idea of dreaming. He says poems are waking dreams, the aristocratic indulgencies of the intellect, the luxuries of otherwise unemployed minds; Milton's Paradise Lost is but a sublime hallucination, Michael Angelo's painting in the Sistine Chapel are elaborated dreams. According to this view of the subject the mind is most spiritualized when least awake. But surely such a conclusion is contrary to reason, for who can believe that voluntary mental abstraction is not associated with vigilance of spirit, or that the exercise of memory and imagination is not compatible with sound judgment? As well may we say that, to look steadily over the past and thence to anticipate the future, is but to dream, and carefully to examine the way we have come and the way we are going, is to prove ourselves sound asleep. Reason acquires her proper dominion by abstraction from the senses, by her use of memory and imagination, or else there is no reality; no truth beyond bodily sensation. It is true that the poetic imagination imbues the commonest cir-

cumstances with a colouring which the vulgar
mind regards as exaggerated, but yet the most
successful exercises of creative genius are remarkable for their philosophic truthfulness, and the
mind which reasons abstractedly, that is while
voluntarily dissociated from the circumstances and
the senses of the body, is most conversant with
the great principles which connect all science, all
art, all moral and all physical relations, with the
truth that commends itself equally to the admiring
understanding and to the convicted conscience as
in the sight of God. Those whom sensualists have
deemed madmen and dreamers, have been the en-
lighteners of their race. They have ascended in
their thoughts out of the sight of the common
down-looking men of this world, and have held their
lamp of life to be relumed at the sun of another
and higher system, which cannot be reached by
telescopes, but is realized by faith.   Divine Wisdom has created the mind of man of too expansive
a nature to be properly limited by the atmosphere
and attractions of earth, and of too inquisitive
and spiritual a capacity to be quite easy in believing only in the properties of matter.   Those persons really dream who see no further than the
surface ; who realize nothing beyond the evidence
of the senses, and read not spiritually the meaning of the grand panorama spread before their
eyes.   But those are vividly and vigorously awake,

who can withdraw themselves from sounds and colours, that they may reflect upon treasured ideas, and interpret the mystery of their existence by enjoying their spiritual faculties, in intercourse with other minds and in communion with their Eternal Parent.

CHAPTER XIII.

THE DIFFERENCE BETWEEN ABSENCE AND ABSTRACTION
OF MIND, AND THEIR RELATIONS TO THE STATE OF
THE WILL IN CONNEXION WITH THE BODY.

IT is well to consider the difference between absence and abstraction of mind. The former is a mere morbid vacuity, a listless habit, or unmeaning dreaminess; the latter, a full and intent occupation. Absence is much known in brown-study and after dinner by the winter fire. It is also common in church and in school, at lectures and at lessons. But mental abstraction is an active and self-absorbing process, in which a powerful and cultivated will sustains the soul in that intellectual exultation which constitutes the habit of true genius. Absence of mind, like sleep, is common to us all, but voluntary abstraction, to the extent which is necessary to great excellence, and for the purpose of enjoying truth or realizing fiction, like the *clairvoyance* of mesmerism, is a rare endowment, by which the possessor dwells, as nearly as may be in consistence with bodily life, in the purer region of the spirit. But there is danger in all sublunary enjoyments. Intellectual objects are often pursued to the very verge of that abyss by which Omnipotence has wisely limited the sphere of human thought, and thus many perish as regards all the proper uses of their present being, while distrust and discontent become stamped upon their features and incorporated with every atom of their substance. By boldly venturing on speculative self-indulgence, they madly leap the bounds of rational inquiry and then quarrel with their God, because he is pleased to surround creation with an outer darkness, in which perverted reason, thus proudly endeavouring to penetrate, becomes involved, perhaps for ever. The history of every age, from that of Eden to the present era, proves that the mental faculties, as well as the grosser appetites to which our fallen nature is subject, require the dominant control of moral and religious principles for their safe and happy exercise. Presumption plucks only evil from the tree of knowledge, while indifference lies blighted even beneath the tree of life.

When a person becomes addicted to the habit of mental absence, he of course becomes more and more infirm of purpose; his will has no employment in the control of his thoughts; his moral as well as mental constitution is on the extreme edge of danger; the total and eternal death of his soul is at hand. The mind cannot be elevated

G 2

above the gross air and night-hag hauntings of
sensuality, nor be endowed with the delight of
true freedom and power, unless objects are set
before it of a spiritual and eternally-enlarging
nature.   If we understand not our relation to
other beings, we lose our interest in them, and
soon cease to be attracted towards them but by
sensual impulses.   Human affection and intellect
both fail of their proper ends, unless reason be
employed in consecutive thought, that is, in comparing facts and deducing truths.   The idle or
absent man is one who thinks not for himself as a
part of a grand community of minds. He cannot
be said to be educated.   If his mind grow, it is
only, like a jungle-creeper, to encumber others.
His busiest thinkings are mere outlines of bodily
sensations.   He owns no claims superior to his
own, no active charities dwell in his heart; his
faith, if he have any, is not, like God's gift, large
and beneficent, as all God's gifts are when duly
exercised, but all his affections are contracted and
centered in his little bodily self. He shrinks from
Christianity; its demands are too great for him, as
it requires intellectual agony and the crucifixion
of the lower self for the regeneration in glory of
the higher self.   There must be the struggling
out of chaos into new creation by the spirit, but
he is satisfied with his own bubble and gazes only
on that till it bursts.   He is miserably weak,

because he has not been obedient to divine law, which would have urged him to triumph over circumstances and selfishness by acting, like a man, with a worthy, because a rational, end in view; for to seek aright for honor and immortality is to coöperate with God.

The man of sequestered habits, indeed, rightly demands our admiration, if, in the voluntary surrender of delightful sociality, the efforts of his soul be directed to the contrivance and accomplishment of means to ameliorate the condition of his fellow man; but the absurd trifler, who prefers absence of mind from feebleness of will, or because in his sickly pride he happens to have disgusted himself with the common business of earth, is unfit for friendship and incapable of love, all his ideas of happiness arise and end in the body, and the proper home of his spirit is the dreary solitude which selfishness creates; for if the body be not kept under by proper employment of mind, reason yields to madness, and the man is driven to the desert or among the tombs by a legion of familiar spirits within him, which can neither be bound nor dispossessed. This is the frequent catastrophe of refusing to act for eternity, by maintaining dominion over the body.

To the will, all knowledge appeals; and to rectify its wandering tendencies, revealed truth addresses our reason and demands our faith. Re-

ligion implies the belief of an unapprehended
series of realities, above our present nature, to
be hoped for and to be attained; because the very
announcement of these truths inspires a desire
that, as it grows, elevates us into the region to
which all true spiritual thought, feeling, and action properly and alone belong. Let us reflect
then, again and again, that the power of directing
the attention by a voluntary process of abstraction
from those objects which invite the senses, for the
purpose of regarding ideas in the memory, constitutes the distinctive characteristic of human
intellect; and that the superiority of one mind
over another is necessarily determined by the
degree in which this gift is granted and is cultivated. The will makes the man, and his future
history hangs on its present state.

When Newton was asked how he discovered the
system of the universe, he answered, "By thinking about it." This thinking to an end, is the
glory of mind. The power of fixing the intellect
on an object, and bringing all facts within our
knowledge, that by possibility relate to that object, to elucidate it; and also the search after
new facts, with a presentiment of their existence,
prove that the human understanding is constituted
in keeping with the mind which contrived the
universe. Perceiving the reason of one fact, the
human intellect correctly infers the reason why

other facts should be found. We find whatever we reasonably look for. We naturally expect consistency; for the plan of Omnipotence agrees with reason, it is pure reason. On this ground the man of sagacity sets himself to think of a subject with a faith in the powers of his mind; a conviction that, by continuing to attend to objects of thought, he will see their connection and relation. Thus one thought awakes ten thousand; and these all move like an army in obedience to one will and to one purpose. By urging our attention with strenuous effort, higher and higher, we triumph over the distractions of sense; and in the calm above, to which the spirit climbs through clouds and Alpine obstacles, the sky appears as that of another world.

"As some strange thoughts transcend our wonted themes,
And into glory peep."—*H. Vaughan.*

Of course the moral perception must precede and guide the intellectual faculty, or otherwise the mind becomes meteoric and uncertain; being excited into action, not according to a choice induced by regard to moral results, but according to accident, or as objects may happen to be more or less pleasing or repulsive. In fact, it appears that, unless the mind be employed in obedient accordance to a higher will than that which be-

longs to itself, education or improvement, except
in a brutal or mechanical sense, is not possible.
Hence the necessity of a conscientious regard to
the dictates of divine will in order to advancement
in the understanding and enjoyment of the highest class of truths,—those which relate to the
proper uses of the body and to spirit, considered
as moral and religious.   Here we see why the
wise of former ages, who possessed a strong reason, although but a feeble glimmering of the
light, which the first tradition shed on the young
world, constantly looked for a coming revelation
concerning future existence ; from which man
might more fully learn his duty towards God, and
thus reach further in his apprehension of immortality, goodness and truth.   Here then we arrive
at the point.   However ingeniously men may
reason concerning the evolution of mind from
matter, they never can reconcile facts with their
theories, nor in any way account for the operations
of consciousness and volition, but by supposing
spiritual existence.   It is however consolatory to
discover, that the more we investigate our mental
and physical nature, the more reason we find to
receive, with implicit faith, the knowledge that is
brought to our minds in the book which bears on
its pages the demonstration of its being the revealed information which the Maker of man con-

descends in mercy to communicate to him, and which, moreover, they who study wisely find to be exactly of the kind they needed.

Without the individual endowment of will we could not feel otherwise than as a part or a property of another being; if, indeed, the very idea of feeling does not imply a distinct personality in that which feels. But we all act, if not with the conviction that we must answer for our deeds to Him who has so variously endowed us, at least with a feeling that we must all individually reap the result of our own conduct, unless Omnipotence interfere with his own laws. None but a being in some measure apprehending the mind of its Maker, can be governed by moral laws, or be made to feel as we all do, from an intuitive conviction, however disobeyed or however condemning, that the law, written on the heart by the finger of God, is holy, just and good. This proves that the human mind acknowledges no lasting relationship with things that perish; for a man that has been taught to love moral truth, cannot afterwards be satisfied with defects: his will and his love must seek for rest in moral perfection and eternal life, that is, in God. We may then well conclude this chapter in the language of Holy Writ, and say, *there is a spirit in man and the inspiration of the Almighty giveth him understanding.* Law and conscience spring not from the dust.

CHAPTER XIV.

THE ACTION OF MIND ON THE NERVOUS ORGANIZATION IN MEMORY, &c.

THE operation of the soul upon the body, and the incorporeal origin and end of mind, will be further rendered manifest by meditating on another endowment, namely, memory. This, indeed, is presupposed in the idea of abstraction; since we cannot contemplate or reflect unless the mind be previously furnished with objects or the remembered images of past impressions. We may dwell the rather on this faculty as it is essential to the exercise of thought, and must precede reasoning. Hesiod said "the nine muses are the daughters of Mnemosyne;" and rightly does he thus determine, since without memory they never could have existed, for every production of human intellect has its origin in this faculty; hence the mind of the rational being is first exercised in examining objects and enjoying sensations, since the remembrance of these constitute the groundwork of reflection and of forethought. The infant's reason requires only familiarity with facts, and the opportunity of comparing them with each other, to become manifest and perfect. Thus it happens that savage tribes and persons wholly without education exhibit so many of the characteristics of childhood.

It is not my purpose to investigate this faculty in philosophical order, but to relate certain facts in connexion with its exercise, which may assist us in deducing further inferences concerning the independence and management of the thinking principle. Attention and association are generally deemed essential to the memory, but experience certainly proves that. its extent or capacity does not entirely depend on what is commonly understood by attention and association. At least we find that, in many instances, we cannot detect the association; nor does it often appear that facility of recollection is in proportion to the effort to attend and to retain, but rather to the suitability of the subject to the mental character and habit of the individual.

A gentleman engaged in a banking establishment made an error in his accounts, and, after an interval of several months, spent days and nights in vain endeavours to discover where the mistake lay. At length, worn out by fatigue, he went to bed, and in a dream recollected all the circumstances that gave rise to the error. He remembered that on a certain day several persons were waiting in the bank, when one individual,

who was a most annoying stammerer, became so
excessively impatient and noisy that, to get rid of
him, his money was paid before his turn, and the
entrance of this sum was neglected, and thus
arose the deficiency in the account.   Now here
we have an instance of memory without association ; because the impression was one of which
there was no consciousness at the time when it
occurred; for the fact on which the case rested
was not his having paid the money but his having
neglected to insert the payment.

Our memory, as available for the common purposes of intelligence, appears to be in proportion
to the interest we take in any subject by nature,
habit or education. We remember most distinctly,
according to the common law of association, those
things which relate to our chosen pursuits, or which
impress us through our keenest and most engrossing affections. We recall even the sufferings of
the body in connexion with some state of our
passions which those sufferings excited. Hence
the injurious effect of tyrannical punishments on
the youthful mind.   Such arbitrary inflictions,
not being accompanied with a moral persuasion
of propriety and kind intention, engender slavish
fear and contempt. The despotic might that
wounds the body merely to enforce its will, is
necessarily despised; and while the body suffers
under it, terror and revenge are the only passions

excited; for gentleness and love alone produce repentance. The passions, excited by the punishment, recur on the remembrance of the pain endured; and thus a repetition of such punishment makes either a coward or a villain, or more probably both; for fear and hatred become the habit of every mind that suffers without the conviction that justice and love are one.

There can be no doubt that ordinarily we best remember what most strongly affects us, either agreeably or otherwise. But this faculty is so variously modified in different individuals, that the effort or the enjoyment, which some find necessary to fix objects upon the mind; others feel to be only impediments to the process. The late Dr. Leyden, who could repeat verbatim a long act of parliament after having once read it, found this kind of memory an inconvenience rather than an advantage, because he could never recollect any particular point in the act without repeating to himself all that preceded the part he required.

The memory of reasoning is strong in proportion to the distinctness of apprehension and the linking together of accordant ideas. We hold most firmly what we grasp most completely. The memory of sensation is generally proportioned to the acuteness of sensation, but a rapid succession of ideas is constantly obliterating previous impressions, by stamping new ones. Yet it appears

from facts that, the impressions always remain
distinct in the mind, and require only a proper
condition to be so perceived and read off in the
order in which they were received. The manner
also in which the acquisition is made, greatly influences the power of retention and of reproduction. Thus, under the urgency of a pressing
occasion, a celebrated actor prepared himself for
a new, long and difficult part, in a surprisingly
short space of time. He performed it with perfect accuracy, but the performance was no sooner
over than every word was forgotten; at least no
effort could recall them, although doubtless they
were retained, and would return to the perception
of the mind under favourable circumstances.

But it should be understood that there are several leading phenomena referable to the head
of memory. There is the simple latent retention
of whatever impression on the senses conveys
to the mind, which constitutes memory strictly
speaking. There is recollection, or the voluntary
reproduction of those impressions, and there is
conception such as the painter or the poet evinces,
who accurately and vividly delineates past occur-
rences, absent friends .and remembered scenes,
with the force of present reality. The performer,
before-mentioned, doubtless possessed the memory
of the part he acted, although he could never
afterwards recall it. He recollected other charac-

ters well, because they were deliberately acquired. The power of memory in connexion with association appears to be influenced by the direction and intensity of the will, that is to the degree and kind of attention required: perhaps the state of our affections has more to do with this faculty than with any other.   Recollection is of vast importance to our common intercourse, but abstract memory is probably more important to the actual education of the soul; since the memory, which is altogether latent and concealed under one set of circumstances, becomes active and useful under another.   Like certain pictures, they appear and disappear according to the direction of the light.

The reproduction of impressions in that exercise or condition of mind called conception, affords very striking evidence that ideas once received are as it were stereotyped on the memory.   They are not painted in fading colours but seem only to require a certain disengagedness of the attention from other objects to be again perceived as vividly as ever.   Thus we see the reason why seclusion and mental abstraction are so naturally sought, when we wish to recall the past, or studiously to review a subject with which we have been familiar.   By voluntary effort we put ourselves into the most favourable position for the retrospect; for we are endowed with a consciousness that the images and perceptions at any time experienced still belong to us, and may again be felt, if the impressions of the present could but be removed from before the eye of mind.   The obstacles to this spiritual sight are often as it were accidentally dissipated, and the past assumes all its pristine reality; a beautiful example of which occurs in the life of Niobuhr, the celebrated Danish traveller, "When old, blind, and so infirm, that he was able only to be carried from his bed to his chair, he used to describe to his friends the scenes which he had visited in his early days with wonderful minuteness and vivacity.   When they expressed their astonishment, he told them that as he lay in bed, all visible objects being shut out, the pictures of what he had seen in the east continually floated before his mind's eye, so that it was no wonder he could speak to them as if he had seen them yesterday.   With like vividness the deep intense sky of Asia, with its brilliant and twinkling host of stars, which he had so often gazed at by night, or its lofty vault of blue by day, was reflected in the hours of stillness and darkness on his inmost soul."*

This may perhaps be considered as an example of the highest degree of healthy conception; that is, the voluntary abstraction of the mind allowing the past to appear in its original order and clear-

* Dr. Abercrombie.

ness. That remarkable phenomenon which drowning persons and others on the verge of death have often been known to experience, belongs to the same property of the soul, for they have described the state of their memories under these mysterious circumstances, as representing the history of their lives, at once and altogether like a vast *tableau vivant*. But, probably, an approach to this sight of our realized existence, more or less confused with our consciousness of the present, is essential to the exercise of memory: a certain state of mind associates past ideas with certain sights and sounds, and we mentally again perceive the past as if present.

Something like this leads to that state on which depends the theory of apparitions or spectral illusions, which seem to be only a more disjointed attention to reality or obliviousness of the present; thus allowing former impressions to re-appear as they occur in dreaming, the senses not being in a state of sufficient activity to prevent ideas from infringing on them.

The following is another illustration of conception, almost as striking as the foregoing. "In the church of St. Peter, in Cologne, the altar piece is a large and valuable picture of Rubens, representing the martyrdom of the Apostle. This picture having been carried away by the French, in 1805, to the great regret of its inhabitants, a painter of that city undertook to make a copy of it from recollection, and succeeded in doing so in such a manner that the most delicate tints of the original are preserved with the most minute accuracy. The original painting has now been restored, but the copy is preserved along with it, and even when they are rigidly compared, it is scarcely possible to distinguish the one from the other."

The images of objects seem to be actually reproduced before the eye of the mind by a voluntary effort, in every exercise of recollection; and, what is very surprising, the images thus reproduced by the will sometimes continue to obtrude themselves, even on the bodily sense, when the mind would fain dismiss them, so as to assume that real appearance of the object thought of, which induces weak-minded persons to think that they have seen supernatural apparitions. Thus a gentleman, mentioned by Dr. Hibbert, having been told of the sudden death of a friend, saw him distinctly when he walked out in the evening. "He was not in his usual dress, but in a coat of a different colour, which he had left off wearing for some months. I could even remark a figured vest which he had worn about the same time, also a coloured silk handkerchief around his neck, in which I had used to see him in the morning."

The power of the mind to embody whatever it

strongly conceives, is strikingly demonstrated in those cases in which a number of persons have imagined themselves to have seen the same apparition. Thus a whole ship's crew were thrown into consternation by the ghost of the cook, who had died a few days before. He was distinctly seen by them all, walking on the water with a peculiar gait by which he was distinguished, one of his legs being shorter than the other. The cook, so plainly recognized, was only a piece of old wreck. In such instances, which are common, it is manifest that the mind so impresses the sense of sight with past realities, that it perceives only what imagination presents.

> " Such tricks hath strong imagination,
> That, if it would but apprehend some joy,
> It comprehends some bringer of that joy ;
> Or, in the night imagining some fear,
> How easy is a bush supposed a bear."—*Shakspeare.*

Now it is clear, from every example of recollection, that ideas do not affix themselves in any structure of the body, for every atom of it is successively removed in the processes of vital action. A man's body does not continue to exist of the same identical materials; therefore it follows, as an inevitable conclusion, that memory is not a record written there; the store of ideas must belong to an independent unchanging being; for

whenever they are reproduced they are found un-
altered, and must therefore have existed in that
which does not change, namely, the undecaying
soul.

Those things which belong to our moral being
most powerfully affect our minds, and most strongly
cleave even to our ordinary memory; and if it
were not so, religious truth could not regenerate
the world. Mr. Moffat, the missionary, says, that
when he had concluded a long sermon to a great
number of African savages, his hearers divided
into companies to talk the subject over. "While
thus engaged my attention was arrested by a sim-
ple-looking young man at a short distance. The
person referred to was holding forth with great
animation to a number of people, who were all
attention. On approaching, I found, to my surprise, that he was preaching my sermon over
again, with uncommon precision and with great
solemnity, imitating as nearly as he could the
gestures of the original. A greater contrast could
scarcely be conceived, than the fantastic figure
and the solemnity of his language: his subject
being eternity, while he evidently felt what he
spoke. Not wishing to disturb him, I allowed
him to finish the recital, and seeing him soon
after, told him, that he could do what I was sure
I could not,—that was, preach again the same
sermon verbatim. He did not appear vain of his

superior memory : 'When I hear anything great,' he said, touching his forehead with his finger, 'it remains there.' "

This anecdote affords us an interesting evidence that memory, in connexion with the intuitive appreciation of vast truths, is characteristic of savage as well as civilized man ; in short, it shows that the mind was created for truth, and to be governed by it. The rapid and immense improvement in the social and religious condition of these and other degraded tribes of mankind, under the persuasive operation of doctrines calculated to direct the will, especially by their hold upon the memory, and thence to inspire the conduct with commanding and ennobling motives, is a beautiful fact ; at once proving the fitness of the Christian doctrines for the moral constitution of man, and the unreasonableness of that philosophy which, in spite of the world's experience, attempts to teach us that the brain of a man must be remodelled before he can be mentally regenerated.   If this be true, what a sudden development of new organs or new activities of brain must have happened in the South Sea Islands, and what a new state of cranium must the sensual atheist experience, who, by a flash of thought, is struck from his elevation of self-conceit and self-adoration into an humble conviction of dependance on his God and Saviour!

Man's spiritual nature is rooted in his knowledge or memory, and as he believes so will he act; as he receives truth, so is he influenced; and truth penetrates like the sword of the Spirit, opening every mind that it strikes for the reception of a world of new realities. Let the will be arrested and the attention fixed to look upon the Gospel, and its grandeur becomes manifest and influential. As, when a man like Newton, having the idea of gravitation forced upon his attention, gradually beholds the universe hanging together and in motion thereby, and makes all his calculations in keeping with that knowledge; so the Christian sees in one grand truth the harmonizing power of all worlds, and calculates only on the force of love as the governing principle of heaven.

A man never forgets, however he may neglect, the truth which he has willingly admitted to his mind as a ruling principle, that is, a truth commended to his conscience. As the poor African said, "When I hear anything great it remains;" so whatever we feel to be morally true will cleave either to torment or to delight us, according to its nature, and according to our felt obedience to the master truths—the demands of God upon our being.

Memory then is not the spontaneous action of an apparatus, like Babbage's calculating machine,

with figures that revolve in endless combination.
It is a state of mind. Mind produces it. Even
those figures, thus revolving and combining,
existed in all their power of infinite reproduction
in the mind that conceived the method of thus
evolving "numbers beyond number numberless,"
from the transpositions and combinations of only
nine remembered units. Thus, perhaps, from the
vast but limited multitude of ideas derived from
the impressions in time, eternity may be filled
with thoughts. The order and happiness resulting from their endless multiplication will depend
on the few regulating principles which God has
given to us in his law, and if this continue to be
broken, the confusion and misery of our spirits
will be as endless as our capacity of thinking.

CHAPTER XV.

THE CONNEXION OF MEMORY WITH THE HABIT AND CON-
DITION OF THE BRAIN, AND THE USE OF THE BODY.

INTIMACY with facts and things in their mutual
influence on each other, constitutes our individual
world of knowledge, and this acquaintance with
circumstances or things, remains in our minds
without a necessary connexion with language.
Ideas must generally be presented by words from
one mind to another in this state of being; but,
that ideas once produced exist in the mind, independently of their conventional associates, is
testified by a great variety of facts, especially in
the history of disease, as it affects the manifestation of the mind; and this it does, more or less,
in every instance, as we have already seen; because what is called health is nothing more than
the state of body best adapted for the exercise
and training of the soul in its intercourse with
the material world. Memory, like all other
mental manifestation, is suspended by pressure
on the brain, and in fact by anything which
powerfully disturbs its functions; hence it is

presumed by some physiologists that memory
has no existence but as a function of the brain,
and many wonderful cases of recovery from ce-
rebral injury, with restoration of this faculty,
are referred to in proof that the brain is the sole
cause of remembrance. The brain of course is
necessary to conscious existence, such as we
experience, and therefore of course it is essential
to memory in connexion with the active manifestation of this life; but yet the very facts which
are quoted as evidences that memory is a function
of the brain, also afford us positive proof that
it is something more.

I knew an intelligent lady, who suddenly lost
all association between ideas and language. She
became as completely destitute of speech as a
new-born infant. Under medical treatment,
however, she gradually recovered ; she again
learned to speak, read, and write, just as a child
learns, until some months after the attack, when
her former information and faculty rapidly returned. She told me that her remembrance of
facts was as clear as ever during this speechless
state,—all she had lost was language. Even her
recollection of music was perfect, and she performed elaborate pieces with her accustomed
skill, although not a single idea in her mind
could present itself in words. She soon after-

H

wards died suddenly of apoplexy, and the cause
of the impediment was then proved to exist in
disease of the brain.

A degree of this disorder occurs when the
brain has suffered from fatigue, as in the case
of Spalding, a celebrated scholar in Germany,
who being called on to write after great exertion
and distraction of mind, found himself incapable .
of proceeding correctly beyond the first two
words. The characters he continued to make
were not what he meant, but he knew not where
the fault lay. His speech failed in the same
manner; he spoke other words than he intended,
although he knew everything around him, and
his senses continued perfect. On resting and
refreshing his nervous system the confusion was
removed.

This loss of association between words and
ideas is often observed in paralytics. It is probable that persons labouring under such malady
are always conscious that the sounds they utter
are unintelligible to those whom they address,
and their distress is greatly aggravated by the
fact. This was the case with the lady just mentioned. Patients are rarely able to give us a
distinct account of their sensations under such
circumstances. Dr. Hollond, however, also relates an instance to the point, in which loss of
memory and articulation of words followed an

accident in an aged gentleman. " He could not remember the names of his servants; nor, when wishing to express his wants to them, could he find right words to do so. He was *conscious* of uttering unmeaning sounds, and reasoned on the singularity at the time, as he afterwards stated." The organs influenced by the will are more or less disordered when the power of recollection is morbidly defective, as in palsy. This disease is accompanied by an unsteadiness and tremor, or rigidity of the muscles, as well as an incapacity of fixing the attention. There is some interference with the muscular sense, by which we prepare ourselves for the use of our other senses.

Here it may not be inappropriate to observe the connexion between attention, memory, and muscular action. All the voluntary activities of our bodies are modified by the state of our memories in relation to our senses, more particularly to the muscular sense, or that feeling by which we regulate our movements in regard to gravitation and avoid danger. Although we seem not to attend to our ordinary muscular actions, yet we really do attend to them and in fact exercise a power of comparison in every intentional movement. We walk according to our experience in the use of our legs and feet, and we handle objects as we have before felt. We balance our muscles instinctively in every effort according to the necessity which former circumstances may have suggested. We take not a cup in our hand without previously preparing ourselves, and the will braces the muscles for the purpose, in keeping with our preconceived notion of the weight of the body to be lifted. Let a person, unacquainted with its weight, attempt to take up a cup of mercury, and he will probably spill its contents. Other complicated and rapid movements of the hand, in the delicate execution of works of art and manufacture, require an apt and ready memory, as well as a well-trained and active hand. An impairment of memory destroys the steady quickness that is required. We find that, in the cotton mills, the activities of the brain are tried to such a degree by steam and ingenuity, that certain movements of the machinery can only be followed by persons possessed of quick memory and corresponding nervous energy; and hence that these parts of the work can only be accomplished or tolerated by individuals from puberty to manhood; because, at that period alone is the association between memory and action sufficiently electric to suit the market.

Mental education improves the grace and expressiveness of the body, at least of the features, to so great an extent as to be commonly acknowledged as a powerful cause of the influence which men maintain over each other. The specific distinction between an educated and an uneducated man is in the power of reflection; the memory of the former having been trained, that of the latter being left wild. This training of memory affects the whole tone, character, and bodily deportment of a man. As a voluntary effort of memory is attended by a peculiar fixedness of the body, and a steadiness of the senses, which are necessary to preserve the attention to associated ideas, the habit of this effort imparts a deliberative expression to the features, and causes even a man's muscular movements to partake of the more measured and sedate tendency of his mind. Hence also it may fairly be concluded, that one who has been accustomed rationally to apply this faculty, is better qualified to control his instincts, to govern his passions, and to regulate all those impulses which spring immediately from his physical constitution. Hence too, natural philosophers, men who remember, collect and think on facts, are less disposed to insanity, than are poets and persons who delight in imagination without an orderly and proper cultivation of memory. In short, proper application of this endowment is the foundation of physical as well as mental and moral improvement. Those nations have the best formed heads who have been possessed of the best histories or traditions, and who have been called to the highest exercise of memory; for in this consists

the principal means of advancing the arts of civilization and of maintaining the dominion of truth
and religion both over mind and body. The very
act of acquiring, recording, or recollecting true
knowledge, is attended by a state of brain and a
sobriety of manner which tend at once to embody,
impersonate, and fix its advantages in the individual so employed, and to perpetuate the benefit
in his offspring. If therefore the increase of
schools did nothing more than demand a general
employment of youthful memory in acquiring
truth, it would accomplish immense good, for
this is always associated more or less with control
of the body, and it will moreover be the groundwork of right reason when coming circumstances
shall require severer exercise of intellect.

CHAPTER XVI.

THE INFLUENCE OF MENTAL HABIT ON THE CHARACTER OF THE MEMORY.

It is remarkable that persons endowed with an energetic and busy imagination have been frequently most defective as regards verbal memory, at least in the power of recollecting words. Thus Rousseau and Coleridge always found it difficult to remember even a few verses, although composed by themselves. The reason seems to be, that their minds quickly caught hold of the ideas expressed and at once associated them with others, much in the same manner that we find delirious persons do under certain conditions of the nervous system; the powers of perception being entire, but the attention being occupied by mental objects rather than sensible ones, as already described under the head of abstraction. The nervous system of such persons is employed in other relations than those best adapted to the use of memory.

The celebrated Porson was a man of a contrary stamp. Recollection was the habit of his mind, and his life was a mixed commentary on profane

and sacred learning, and his genius was like a
phosphorescence on the graves of the dead. It
is said of him that nothing came amiss to his
memory." He would set a child right in his two-
penny fable book, repeat the whole of the moral
tales of the Dean of Badajoz, a page of Athenæus
on cups, or of Eustathius on Homer. He could
bring to bear at once on any question every passage from the whole range of Greek literature
that could elucidate it; and approximate on the
instant the slightest coincidence in thought or
expression; and the accuracy was quite as surprising as the extent of his recollection." This facility
was the result of early and continued habit.

Dr. Arnold had a remarkable memory. He
quoted from Dr. Priestley's Lectures on History,
when in the professor's chair at Oxford, from the
recollection of what he had only read when no
more than eight years of age. His memory extended to the exact state of the weather on particular days, or the exact words and position of
passages which he had not seen for twenty years.
This faculty was more particularly acute on subjects of history and geography, from the early
habit of exercising it on these subjects; having
been taught to go accurately through the stories
of the pictures and portraits of the successive
English reigns before he was eight years old, and
being at that age accustomed to recognize at a

glance the different counties of a dissected map of England.

The power of memory, provided the brain be in a healthy state, will be proportioned to the determination with which an individual attends to the subject he would remember; that is, in proportion to the motive. If fancy interfere, memory is disturbed. This strength of purpose has always characterized those who have been celebrated for power of memory, and this will of course mainly arise from the feeling of importance which habit or teaching may attach to the object in view. Thus Cyrus is said to have learned the name of every soldier in his army, that he might be able to command them the better; and Mithridates, for the same reason, became acquainted with the languages of the twenty-two nations serving under his banners. It is stated by Eusebius that Esdras restored the sacred Hebrew Volumes by memory, when they had been destroyed by the Chaldeans. St. Anthony, the Egyptian hermit, could not read, but knew all the Scriptures by heart from having heard them. Pope Clement V. impaired his memory from a fall on the head; but by dint of application he recovered its powers so completely, that Petrarch informs us that he never forgot anything that he had once perused.

Are we to conclude that this principle of the mind assumes varieties of manifestation, according to the facility which different conformations of brain or sense afford; or are we to infer that mind is created with diversified degrees and kinds of this capacity? Facts point to the conclusion that the manifestation of memory is modified by the state of the nervous system in relation to the power of attending. Hence memory is matured by habit; for, in order to a perfect reminiscence, the mind must act upon the nervous organization in such a manner as to excite in it a sense of the images recalled. This is sometimes so powerfully excited, that we unintentionally imitate in our action that which we would describe. Circumstantial signs are associated in our ideas, and they often produce the effect, not only in our minds but in our features. Thus Descartes, being fondly in love with a girl who squinted, never spoke of her without squinting.

If the brain be occupied or excited by disease, or distracted by mental perturbation, the will has but little power in directing the attention either to the recollection of past impressions or to the observation of things present. A man is then said to be discomposed; the healthy order of his thoughts is broken, his memory is confused, his attention disturbed.

The habit of using the mind in any particular direction, or on any class of objects, gives a prominence and readiness to that part of the nervous system which is called into exercise, and therefore the memory employed in daily reasoning is facile in proportion to habit, as long as we continue in health. The habit of mind then actually alters the condition and power of the instruments of mental manifestation; and, within certain limits, qualifies it for use, according to the extent and kind of demand made upon it; thus proving, beyond controversy, that ordinary memory depends on mental determination in the use of a healthy organization. The power itself originates in that which attends, intends, wills, and not in that which is acted on by the will. Seeing then that mental confusion arises from inaptitude of the brain, as relates to the senses under the action of the will, we may fairly conclude that when the will shall act only in that which retains ideas, and deals with pure memory, there will be no confusion, but that all experienced facts will stand clearly in their exact order as originally presented. As we advance in this subject we shall discover further reason for this conclusion.

However excellent the development of a man's brain may be, he will be incapable of exercising his faculties to good purpose unless he is habituated to their control under the excitement of moral motives. The brain does not respond to the demands of reason but by degrees. It is not brought into a state suitable to the proper manifestation of our faculties but by long habits. In fact the brain is not fully developed, as the instrument or medium of intellect, unless the mind have been regularly educated and drawn out by appropriate employment during the period of its growth. The will, in exercising attention while acquiring knowledge and in reflection, that is, in using memory, really produces such a change in the size and order of the nervous fibrils of the brain, as to render it better and better adapted for use, as long as the laws of its formation allow or until disease interfere. We find then, instead of mind and memory resulting from brain, that brain, as far as it has relation to the mind, is developed and regulated in subserviency to the will; for however good the natural formation of a child's brain may be, he must grow up an idiot if his will be not called into action by moral influences; that is, by sympathy with other spirits. The histories of Caspar Hauser, Peter the wild boy, and others, elucidate this subject and confirm this conclusion.

The desperate shifts to which materialists are driven to avoid an acknowledgment of spiritual existence, appears most palpably in their endeavours, physiologically, to account for memory. They say, sensation is the only source of faculty. But then they fail to show what experiences sensation. They add, sensation would be sterile, unproductive of will and memory, if it did not remain impressed on the tissue of the brain, so as to be found after many years. All we see, hear, feel, taste, conceive,—is, say they, incorporated and constitutes part and parcel of our brains. What "a book and volume" a well-stored brain must be, all alive with indelible sensations! This theory, like many others, is indebted to poetry rather than logic, and it certainly was stolen from Shakspeare, who makes Hamlet thus philosophically promise the ghost of his royal father :—

> " Yea, from the table of my memory
> I'll wipe away all trivial fond records ;
> All saws of books, all forms of pleasures past,
> That youth and observation copied there ;
> And thy commandment all alone shall live
> Within the book and volume of my brain,
> Unmix'd with baser matter."

But it is surmised that the great dramatist intended, in the character of Hamlet, to represent a philosophical, poetical madman; and this theory of memory certainly appears well to become such a character; especially as he, at the same time, attributes a supremacy to the individual's will which it does not and cannot possess; for however we may desire it, to wipe away the record, however fond or trivial, is impossible, although we may indeed become for a time unconscious of its exist-

ence by a full occupation of the mind on new
objects of thought.

It must, however, be acknowledged, that the
material hypothesis of memory has been presented
in so beautiful a manner as to fascinate, if not to
satisfy, the understanding.   We need not be surprised at the almost infinite ideas which may be
interwoven into the fibrils of the brain, since
microscopic observers assure us that the smallest
visible point of its substance is not more than the
1-8000th of an inch in diameter, it is therefore
estimated that 8000 ideas may be represented on
every square inch of the thinking nerve-matter;
so that, considering the large surface of such
matter in man, he may be supposed in this manner
capable of receiving some millions of simple ideas
or impressions.   It seems vain to say, as do some
advocates of this notion, that such broad methods
of accounting for ideas do not favour materialism.
Surely, if ideas exist only in the brain and spinal
marrow, to die is to lose them.   But let us enquire what is an idea?   It is a mind-act, which cannot be but in a conscious being.   Something
more than atoms must be required for the production and recognition of our mental impressions; something consenting—besides brain.   As
images on the retina are not ideas until a man
attend to them, for he does not see them while his
mind is intently engaged about other things, so

whatever may exist actively or passively in the brain, affects not the consciousness till the mind is in correspondence with it. Conceive a man, say Milton, using imagination, memory, judgment, day after day, until the body is no longer convenient. He choses, observe, to "justify the ways of God to man," but he does not meditate on knowledge really belonging to *himself*, but on the play of nerve-fibrils, which put him in mind of the past and present; for they in fact *contain* all his ideas, all his works, his experience, emotions, affections, thoughts. Now, if such be true, what was Milton when his body died? Is there no answer? Yes! As that immortal spirit, when present in a commodious body saw the "Paradise Lost" in the light which shone amidst his darkness, so that same spirit, endowed with larger love and liberty and intellect, walks with God in the "Paradise Regained." His knowledge and in-wrought history did not perish in the grave.

Supposing that sensation and ideas were capable of being engraved, or cast, or daguereotyped on the leaves of the brain, the question still returns, what perceives them there? The only possible answer is supplied in the Sacred Scripture: "No man knoweth the things of a man, but the spirit of man which is in him." The recurrence of the same ideas is only the recurrence of the same state in that which thinks, but of course the same state in ordinary manifestation implies the return of similar relations with regard to objects of attention. To experience exactly the same state of mind, we must exactly recall the past impressions in their original order, or we must be placed again in precisely the same circumstances in regard to the brain and the senses. A case will illustrate this observation. It may be found at full in the "Assembly Missionary Magazine." The Reverend William Tennant, while conversing in Latin with his brother, fainted and apparently died. His friends were invited to his funeral; but his physician, examining the body, thought he perceived signs of life: he remained in this state of suspended animation for three days longer, when his family again assembled to the funeral, and, while they were all sitting around him, he gave a heavy groan and was gradually restored. Some time after his resuscitation he observed his sister reading: he asked what she had in her hand. She answered "a Bible:" he replied, "what is a Bible?" He was found to be totally ignorant of every transaction of his past life. He was slowly taught again to read and write, and afterwards began to learn Latin under the tuition of his brother. One day while he was reciting a lesson from "Cornelius Nepos," he suddenly felt a shock in his head. He could then speak the Latin fluently as before his illness, and his memory was in all respects completely restored. His brain was no longer so diseased or disordered in its circulation as to prevent his mind from returning to its former relations. Objects again excited their appropriate associations with recorded ideas, and he recollected what he previously knew; his will was as capable of acting on his brain as it did when acquiring Latin at first, his nervous system was again obedient.

CHAPTER XVII.

THE CONNEXION OF MEMORY WITH DOUBLE CONSCIOUSNESS.

ALTHOUGH memory is evinced in very different degrees and under various modifications in different individuals, we must not conclude that this endowment is essentially diversified in its nature and extent, as it appears to be. Many facts tend to prove, that persons may possess large stores of recorded impressions without being aware of it. Perhaps every image or idea received through the senses is really so preserved that, under circumstances yet to come, they may each and every one be perceived and recognized in their proper connexion with each other, so as to enable the corrected and unclouded reason hereafter to read the wisdom and providence of God as permanently written in the minutest circumstances of each one's experience, to discern distinctly the eternal contrariety between truth and falsehood, good and evil; to trace their operation on the mind, to perceive how the human will is rendered responsible by knowledge, and how hopes and efforts are excited by mental associations, and, conse-

quently, how just and beautiful is the royal law
of loving our neighbours as ourselves.   In short
we máy hereafter be able to understand the force
of circumstances in the development of character,
the full weight of education and accountableness,
and from the intelligence growing out of the feeling and reflection of the past, to converse without
restraint with higher or more advanced intelli-
gences, and to exercise our faculties aright in new
and loftier regions, where we shall learn that our
living spirits have been exposed in this world of
trial and darkness to nothing accidental, to nothing trivial; but that other spirits have been
permitted to be busy with our sensations and ideas
for specific purposes of temptation, in just relation
to our own moral state, for spiritual exaltation,
or even, may we not say, for the more mysterious
abandonment of the soul to evil; thereby the
better to exhibit the awful sublimity of divine
government, 'which will ultimately subdue to the
vengeance of love the most opposing elements,
and render darkness itself the medium of glory.

We know that persons may, during sleep and
in certain conditions of disease, exercise a memory of which they are wholly unconscious in
their waking hours, or while enjoying ordinary
health; in short, a memory which has no purpose
in connexion with present existence.

There is an illustrative case related by Dr. Dyce,

of Aberdeen. The patient was an ignorant servant girl, and the affection began with fits of sleepiness, which came suddenly upon her. After these paroxysms had been frequently renewed, she began to talk a great deal during their continuance, without being sensible of anything that was passing about her. In this state she on one occasion distinctly repeated the baptismal service of the Church of England, and concluded with an extemporary prayer. In her case a circumstance was remarked, which in other instances has also been observed, namely, that she perfectly recollected during the paroxysm what took place in former paroxysms, though she had no remembrance of it during the intervals. This is exactly what occurs in many cases of insanity and delirium. I have frequently conversed with persons under both forms of disorder, during fits of excitement, and have found them perfectly at home concerning fancies and impressions which passed before their minds while conversing with me in previous paroxysms; but, in their lucid periods, their whole existence during the fits was quite a blank to them.

Dr. Pritchard mentions a lady who was liable to sudden attacks of delirium. They often commenced while she was engaged in interesting conversation; and on such occasions it happened that, on her recovery from the state of delirium, she instantly recurred to the conversation she was engaged in at the time of the attack. To such a degree was this carried on, that she could even complete an unfinished sentence. During one paroxysm she would pursue the train of ideas which had occupied her mind in a former fit.

The human spirit uses the brain as long as this organ is fit for its purposes, and therefore conscious associated memory is the result of mental action on the brain; and whenever the thinking principle is remembering and directed to the body and its senses, there is probably a reproduction of that very state of nerve or of brain which accompanied the first impression of each remembered idea; and, probably, the brain being again put in the same condition or nearly so, by any cause, as for instance by a stimulus, would facilitate the act of the mind in recalling any impression which had occurred in a similar state of brain; because a return of this state is necessary while mind is acting with the senses.

Dr. Abercrombie relates the following case, on the authority of a respectable clergyman of the Church of England, which aptly illustrates this point. A young woman of the lower rank, aged 19, became insane. She was gentle, and applied herself eagerly to various operations. Before her insanity, she had learned to read and form a few letters, but during her insanity she taught herself to write perfectly, though all attempts to teach her had failed, as she could not attend. She had intervals of reason, which frequently continued for three weeks or longer, during which she could neither write nor read; but immediately on the return of her insanity, she recovered her power of writing and reading perfectly.

Other cases might be related, on the best authority, in which individuals have, during one state, retained all their original knowledge, but during the other state, that only which had been acquired after the first attack. The following history, abbreviated from Dr. Abercrombie's statement, will further illustrate the fact that memory, as well as other faculties, may exist to a greater extent than our ordinary use of recollection would warrant us to suppose. A girl, seven years of age, employed in tending cattle, was accustomed to sleep in an apartment next to one which was frequently occupied by an itinerant fiddler, who was a musician of considerable skill, and who often spent a part of the night in performing pieces of a refined description. These performances were noticed by the child only as disagreeable noises. After residing in this house for six months she fell into bad health, and was removed by a benevolent lady to her own home; where, on her recovery, she was employed as a servant. Some years after she came to reside with this lady, the wonder of the family was strongly excited by hearing the most beautiful music during the night, especially as they spent many waking hours in vain endeavours to discover the invisible minstrel. At length the sound was traced to the sleeping room of the girl, who was fast asleep, but uttering from her lips sounds exactly resembling those of a small violin. On farther observation it was found, that after being about two hours in bed, she became restless and began to mutter to herself; she then uttered tones precisely like the tuning of a violin, and at length, after some prelude, dashed off into elaborate pieces of music, which she performed in a clear and accurate manner, and with a sound not to be distinguished from the most delicate modulations of that instrument. During the performance she sometimes stopped, imitated the re-tuning her instrument, and then began exactly where she had stopped in the most correct manner. These paroxysms occurred at irregular intervals, varying from one to fourteen or even twenty nights; and they were generally followed by a degree of fever. After a year or two her music was not confined to the imitation of the violin, but was often exchanged for that of a piano, which she was accustomed to hear in the house where she now lived; and she then also began to sing, imitating exactly the voices of several ladies of the family. In another year from this time she began to talk a great deal in her sleep, in which she seemed to fancy herself instructing a younger companion. She often descanted with the utmost fluency and correctness on a great variety of topics, both political and religious; the news of the day, the historical parts of scripture, of public characters, of members of the family, and of their visitors. In these discussions she showed the most wonderful discrimination; often combined with sarcasm, and astonishing powers of memory. Her language through the whole was fluent and correct, and her illustrations often forcible and even eloquent. She was fond of illustrating her subjects by what she called a fable, and in these her imagery was both appropriate and elegant. "She was by no means limited in her range—Buonaparte, Wellington, Blucher, and all the kings of the earth, figured among the phantasmagoria of her brain; and all were animadverted upon with such freedom from restraint as often made me think poor Nancy had been transported into Madame Genlis's Palace of Truth." She has been known to conjugate correctly Latin verbs, which she had probably heard in the school-room of the family, and she was once heard to speak several sentences very correctly in French, at the same time stating that she heard them from a foreign gentleman. Being questioned on this subject when awake, she remembered having seen this gentleman, but could not repeat a word of what he said. During her paroxysms it was almost impossible to awake her, and when her eyelids were raised and a candle brought near her eye, the pupil seemed insensible to the light.

During the whole period of this remarkable affection, which seems to have gone on for at least ten or eleven years, she was, when awake, a dull and awkward girl, very slow in receiving any instruction, though much care was bestowed upon her; and, in point of intellect, she was much inferior to the other servants of the family. She showed no kind of turn for music, and had not any recollection of what passed during her sleep.

We are not surprised to find that this singular and interesting girl afterwards deviated from the path of virtue and became insane. The surprise is, that those persons who exhibited kindness to her in the early history of her life, should have abandoned her when disposed to self-abandonment. This is not the manner of a true christian spirit, which exerts itself to counteract ignorance and delusion, and deems those most pitiable and most worthy of watchful care, who are farthest removed from the enjoyment of truth and purity. She had evidently laboured under disease of the brain, especially that part which is influenced by the higher intellectual faculties; therefore the greater should have been the care of her friends

I

to protect her from the persuasions of sensual temptation, which always becomes mighty in proportion to the development of the animal propensities, unless controlled by motives derived from superior knowledge and expectations.

Double consciousness is curiously tested in the case of a person who cannot preserve attention to his body, or to things around him, in consequence of being overpowered by fatigue. He sits, we will suppose, in some uneasy position, not allowing him to resign himself to sleep, but keeping him in a state of alternation between imperfect sleeping and waking; so that he is constantly correcting the aberrations of consciousness that occur in the mind, when the will ceases to act on the senses, by the returning consciousness of his situation when slightly roused. Here the individual recognizes the double mode of his existence, and in the course of a few minutes passes several times from the one state to the other, dreaming one instant and reasoning the next. However the fact may be explained, he is conscious of transition and loses not the sense of his identity, although the memory associated with the exercise of the senses is distinctly seen to differ from that which exists during their suspense; for, in reality, the perceptions of the difference between the objects of the memory in the dreaming and in the wakeful conditions, constitutes all by which the mind knows the difference between sleep and vigilance.

When the exercise of memory is disordered, as, for instance, by disease of the brain, it is often difficult for the patient to awake to the consciousness of realities; and he is apt, as in cases of insanity, to blend the memory of dreams with the impressions of objects on his senses; or even, while apparently gazing at a real scene, to be attending only to an imaginary or remembered one. This state was exemplified in the case of an aged gentleman, whose remarkable affection was lately the subject of public inquiry, and who, while looking out of a window on a wide prospect in England, described it to his housekeeper as a scene in Barbadoes, where he had an estate, and the different parts of that estate he pointed out very minutely. This individual suffered from disease which often rendered him incapable of comparing ideas with present impressions, or dreaming with wakefulness, and of course rendered his memory almost as uncertain when awake as when in a dream.

CHAPTER XVIII.

FURTHER FACTS AND OBSERVATIONS IN PROOF OF THE IMMATERIAL NATURE OF MEMORY.

WE daily experience the recurrence of past impressions to be entirely independent on the will, and we are often surprised at the distinctness with which scenes that had long been lost in oblivion suddenly reappear without the possibility of our detecting the cause of their revival. That such resurrections of thought and impression result from some constant law of our existence, there cannot be a doubt; but that the recognized influence of association is insufficient for the purpose of explaining the fact, we possess abundant proof, in those examples of renewed recollection or its loss, which are so common in consequence of disease. Sir Astley Cooper relates the case of a sailor who was received into St. Thomas's Hospital, in a state of stupor, from an injury in the head, which had continued some months. After an operation he suddenly recovered, so far as to speak, but no one in the hospital understood his language. But a Welsh milk-woman, happening to come into the ward, answered him, for he spoke Welsh, which was his native language. He had, however, been absent from Wales more than thirty years, and previous to the accident had entirely forgotten Welsh, although he now spoke it fluently, and recollected not a single word of any other tongue. On his perfect recovery, he again completely forgot his Welsh and recovered his English.

An Italian gentleman, mentioned by Dr. Rush, in the beginning of an illness spoke English; in the middle of it, French; but, on the day of his death, spoke only Italian. A Lutheran clergyman, of Philadelphia, informed Dr. Rush that Germans and Swedes, of whom he had a large number in his congregation, when near death, always prayed in their native languages; though some of them, he was confident, had not spoken them for fifty or sixty years. An ignorant servant girl, mentioned by Coleridge, during the delirium of fever, repeated, with perfect correctness, passages from a number of theological works in Latin, Greek, and Rabbinical Hebrew. It was at length discovered that she had been servant to a learned clergyman, who was in the habit of walking backward and forward along a passage by the kitchen, and there reading aloud his favourite authors.

Dr. Abercrombie relates the case of a child, four years of age, who underwent the operation of trepanning while in a state of profound stupor from a fracture of the skull. After his recovery, he retained no recollection either of the operation or the accident; yet, at the age of fifteen, during the delirium of a fever, he gave his mother an exact description of the operation, of the persons present, their dress, and many other minute particulars. Dr. Pritchard mentions a man who had been employed with a beetle and wedges, splitting wood. At night he put these implements in the hollow of an old tree, and directed his sons to accompany him the next morning in making a fence. In the night, however, he became mad. After several years his reason suddenly returned, and the first question he asked was, whether his sons had brought home the beetle and wedges. They, being afraid to enter into an explanation, said they could not find them; on which he arose, went to the field where he had been to work so many years before, and found in the place where he had left them, the wedges and the iron rings of the beetle, the wooden part having mouldered away.

It is a remarkable fact that, in many instances, disorder of faculty, more particularly of memory, having resulted from extensive organic disease of the brain, yet individuals so afflicted have, nevertheless, had lucid intervals and a perfect restoration of memory. This has been so marked in some cases, as to have induced the hope of recovery when death has been near at hand, and

has even rapidly ensued, from the increase of the
very disease which led to the mental incapacity.
Mr. Marshall relates, that a man died with a
pound of water in his brain, who, just before
death, became perfectly rational, although he had
been long in a state of idiocy. Dr. Holland refers
to similar cases, and I have witnessed one. Now,
unless we conclude that mind has been recreated
on such occasions, in accommodation to the organic defects, we must conclude that the mind
exists in its integrity, when once formed, distinct
as the light of heaven; though, like it, subject to
eclipse and cloud in its earthly manifestations.

Many such cases might be adduced, but the
foregoing facts suffice to prove that, though a
healthy condition of the brain is essential to the
proper manifestation of mind in this state of being,
or in keeping with the use of the senses, yet that
a history of events lies hidden in the soul, which
only requires suitable excitement and appropriate
circumstances to cause it to be unfolded to the
eye of the mind, in due order, like a written roll.
And, moreover, these facts indicate that our bodies
and our minds are mercifully constituted, in
mutual fitness and accommodation to each other
and the world we dwell in. They also show that,
the active employment of the will, and bodily
health with diversified bodily engagements, are
the best means of correcting that tendency to

mental absence which precedes and accompanies insanity. Moreover, these cases, as well as many others equally well authenticated, "furnish proofs and instances that relics of sensation may exist for an indefinite time in a latent state, in the very same order in which they were originally impressed." Indeed, activity and intensity of all mental power seems to depend on the removal of bodily impediment. At least we see that certain states of body allow the mind to act, without the consciousness of difficulty or effort. Thus Dr. Willis relates the case of a gentleman, who expected his fits of insanity with impatience, because of the facility with which he then exercised his memory and imagination. He said "every thing appeared easy to me. No obstacles presented themselves either in theory or practice. My memory acquired, all of a sudden, a singular degree of perfection. Long passages of Latin authors occurred to my mind. In general, I have great difficulty in finding rythmical terminations, but then I could write verses with as great facility as prose." I knew a clergyman, of fine intellect, who was remarkable for fits of hesitancy in preaching; but who, in his dreams, was accustomed to express himself with intense and most fluent eloquence. Dr. Haycock, professor of medicine, in Oxford, would give out a text, and deliver a good sermon on it, in his sleep, but was incapable of such discourse when awake. A writer in *Frazer's Magazine* mentions a lady, who performed every part of the Presbyterian service in her sleep. Some of her sermons were published. They consist principally of texts of scripture appropriately strung together.

In the *Edinburgh Journal of Science*, a lady is described as being subject to disease, during which she repeated great quantities of poetry in her sleep, and even *capped* verses for half an hour at a time, never failing to quote lines beginning with the final letter of the preceding, till her memory, or rather her brain was exhausted.

We cannot rationally suppose that the peculiar states of the brain, under which memory has thus recurred, acted in any other way than either as a stimulus or medium of action to something always ready to act. These facts, therefore, contribute to make it probable that all thoughts are in themselves imperishable; "yea, in the very nature of a living spirit, it may be more possible that heaven and earth should pass away, than that a single thought should be loosened or lost from that living chain of causes, to all whose links, conscious or unconscious, the free will,—our only absolute itself,—is co-extensive and co-present."*

How awful is the conviction, that the book of judgment is that of our life, in which every idle

* Coleridge.

i 3

word is recorded ; and that no power but His who
made the soul can obliterate our ideas and our
deeds from our remembrance, or blot out trans-
gressions and purify our spirits from the actual
indwelling of evil thoughts !

Every individual experience amply testifies that
the forgotten incidents of long past years, require
only the touch of the kindling spirit to start up,
in all their pristine freshness, before us.   How
often do we remember having recognised in our
dreams, those feelings and circumstances which
had been lost to our waking consciousness, in the
accumulated events which passing time had impressed upon our minds !   And although we cannot say that we acknowledge, as belonging to our
own actual experience, all the visionary combinations which are thus presented to our notice in
dreams, we yet feel that every object in them is
familiar to our knowledge.   Some persons, as we
have said, on the near approach of death have
spoken of the incidents of their lives as being
simultaneously presented before them as if in a
magic mirror, every line as if fixed upon a tablet
by the light, exactly as that revealing light fell on
it.   The portrait of the soul is the perfect reflection of itself, and every man must see his own
character thus for ever visible to the eye of God,
and, probably, hereafter to angels and to men.

The present consciousness of life is but a condition of mind, and our enjoyments are but expressions of the state of our wills; therefore a change of state makes no alteration in our characters, but serves only to exhibit them in new aspects. Thus variety of circumstances tests the stability of our moral principles; but these can be modified only by the relation in which the soul stands with regard to God, the source of moral law; for death is but a change of state, not of moral character.

In connexion with this subject it is interesting to remember that immediately preceding death the mind is commonly occupied about those things with which it has been most intimate during health. Thus Napoleon's last words were " Head "—" Army." Those of a celebrated judge were " Gentlemen of the jury, you are discharged." Cardinal Beaufort cried, " What, no bribing death ! "

Reason and revelation agree then, in asserting, that absolute forgetfulness, or obliteration, is impossible; and that all the events of our history are written in our living spirits; and, whether seen or unseen, will there remain for ever, unless removed by the act of a merciful Omnipotence ! It is true that a thousand incidents will spread a veil between our present consciousness and the record on the soul, but there the record rests waiting the judgment of God. These sublime facts deeply warn us as to the manner in which we suffer our faculties to be engaged, not only as their exercise affects ourselves, but also in their influence on the destiny of others.

Viewing the subject then, both physiologically and metaphysically, we must infer that memory has relation to another mode of existence; and that though, as regards this sphere of being, recollection is greatly influenced by the will, yet that much lies stored in latency, which can only be called into exercise under coming circumstances, when the will shall be more largely endowed, in a manner corresponding with its new relations, and thus be enabled to connect new facts with past impressions. The reasoning and undisturbed spirit shall then understand the meaning of all associated knowledge, and memory shall preserve within us a consciousness of all we have experienced through this life, and add it to that which is to come. Memory indeed seems intended to qualify us to treasure impressions in all worlds, and to carry on the record and history of our feelings from time to eternity. But if the experience of earth is to be our all, then memory is without a sufficient purpose. Is death indeed to end the scene in perpetual oblivion? Is knowledge itself, though the result of a laborious life of attention and of effort, to close for ever, like a beautiful symphony, significant of richer harmony to come, but yet terminating, we know not why, in abrupt and eternal silence? Is the stream to be lost, not in ocean, but in nothing? No. The everlasting future grows upon the past; remembrance is the basis of eternal knowledge. In fact, the full purpose of any one of our intellectual endowments does not appear to be fulfilled in the limited and broken exercise which is afforded to it in the present stage of being, since the utmost advantage we derive from the employment of our faculties now, is to become religious, that is, to be re-bound to the worship and enjoyment of God. Can it be that this re-binding of the prodigal soul to the Eternal Father is only for death, like the victim bound to the altar, to be sacrificed and consumed to ashes, from which no Phœnix-life arises?

Our best ratiocination, under the stimulus of the highest and purest affections, is only an ability to reason from things past to things future, and from experience to analogy; thence obtaining the promise, the desire, the assurance of enlarged capacity for understanding and blessedness; since hope and doubt, in equal balance, are otherwise the only ends of our utmost knowledge here. But expectation and inquiry are purposeless, if there be not a futurity in the mind of God for us, which shall illuminate the chaos and satisfy the trustful soul. Can it be that our Maker has given us a life so rich in promise and excitation merely to terminate in a question that must receive no answer? Is it not most consonant with simple reason as well as with revelation (which is God's response to reason), to believe that our holy desires are properly directed forward to coming events for their fruition; and that what we know, or think we know, now, is intended only to excite our longing for the larger knowledge reserved for hereafter. God is not the God of the dead, but of the living; for all who live for Him live in Him—the life itself; and what we taste of life in this world is but the covenant and agreement of God with our spirits,—a covenant that cannot be broken.

As we cannot believe that Omnipotence ever created even an atom of matter and afterwards annihilated it, so we cannot believe that mind and spirit, created in his own likeness, capable of communion with Himself, and so far partaking of his own nature, should ever perish. Every impression, every idea, every sensation has a place in the individuality of every soul's experience, and is appropriate and necessary to the growth and edification of that soul, and cannot be destroyed without the undoing of the work which Divine Wisdom and power have accomplished; so that to suppose a human being annihilated, or any part of his experience for ever blotted out, is to imagine providence without a purpose, and omniscient wisdom without an object or an end worthy of

human creation.   And are not the facts we have
related concerning attention and memory in perfect agreement with this conclusion of our reason ?
Here then let us pause and ponder on the wonders of our mental and moral being, and the vast-
ness of our destiny as the offspring of the Everlasting Father.

END OF FIRST PART.

THE

POWER OF THE SOUL OVER THE BODY.

PART II.

THE INFLUENCE OF MENTAL DETERMINATION AND EMOTION OVER THE BODY.

THE POWER

OF

THE SOUL OVER THE BODY.

CHAPTER I.

THE POSITIVE ACTION OF THE MIND ON THE BODY, ASSERTED AND EXEMPLIFIED IN THE EFFECTS OF EXCESSIVE AT-TENTION.

PHYSIOLOGY teaches us, by a multitude of facts, that every atom of the animal structure is sub-jected to perpetual change; and that every motion, every action of the body, is the consequence of alteration in the vital condition of one or more of its parts. Not a thought, not an idea, not an affection or feeling of the mind can be excited without positive change in the brain and in the secretions; for every variation in the state of the whole, or any portion, of the nervous system, is of course accompanied by a correspondent change in those organs and functions which it furnishes with energy.

The body can be influenced only by four kinds of force,—chemical, mechanical, vital, and mental.

Health and enjoyment may be destroyed mechanically, as by a blow. Anything which acts chemically may also injure the body, as fire. No arguments can be required to show that the life of the body is maintained in spite of a constant tendency to death; that is, the resident life is incessantly counteracting the common chemical and mechanical influences which are around it. Decomposition and decay commence the moment life leaves the body. So then life appears to be a distinct power. But what is it? We know not. It is neither tangible nor visible. It cannot be weighed nor tested. Like the soul, it is discoverable only by its effects on chemical and mechanical agents. It is not the production of the body, for without it the body itself could not have commenced. It operates on one body, through another, so as to produce a third. It is something capable of being communicated, and is probably independent on organization, at least some fluids are imbued with it. The purpose of vitality, as regards man, is to bring inert matter into such relations to the mind as that the mind may be developed through it, by making physical organization subservient to consciousness and volition. Life is the source of the body's growth, preservation, and reproduction. It exhibits itself in modifying the action of external influences, and by the evolution of new forms under the power of impregnation. But the mind acts as clearly and distinctly on the body as either chemical, mechanical, or vital agency; therefore the mind must possess a distinct existence, action, and force, capable of being superadded to life as life is to matter. Mind, in fact, is the mightiest power we know, and perhaps, properly speaking, the ouly power. Chemical action is but relative, and the result of some power constantly ready to act on matter according to circumstances. Sulphuric acid and potash combine when brought into contact under ordinary circumstances, because something produces a reciprocal change in their particles when within a certain distance of each other; but this change is prevented altogether by causing a galvanic current to influence these bodies, and sulphuric acid may thus be passed through a solution of potash without their combining. We see then that chemical action is dependent on electrical action, and electrical action is dependent on some superior power; the same, it may be, as that which causes gravitation, magnetism, polarity, heat, light, and which pervades all elements; a power which cannot be called material, and which obeys only that will which evoked the universe and still sustains it. In short, all power may be traced up directly to the mind that created and manages all things.

This view of the action of matter may easily be

carried on to a comparison with that of mind;
for we at once perceive the reasonableness of con-
cluding that created mind, as well as matter, may
exist in a quiescent state until brought into relation with certain arrangements and conditions of
matter, or with other minds, according to affinities and laws which operate only under the direct
influence of some superior all-pervading power.
Such a notion is consistent with the facts within
our knowledge, and brings us at once to the necessity of acknowledging our total dependance,
for all the purposes of our being, on the will that
wisely and benevolently determines how and when
we shall feel, so that under one set of circumstances we shall be unconscious, and under another be thoroughly kindled with emotion.

We have already observed the power of the will
in directing and enforcing the motions of the
muscles, but if we further reflect on the various
ways in which will operates, we shall not fail to
be struck with the vast extent of its influences;
not only over the muscles, but also over the source
of bodily life itself, for its exercise modifies the
action both of the brain and the heart; taking
possession, so to speak, of the fountains of energy,
and regulating in some measure the supply of
blood and life to different parts of the body. This
is said not merely of the ordinary power of emotion, but of voluntary employment of the body;

not of sudden impulse, but of steady purpose, such as the determined student or the artist evinces in his patient labor with the book, the pen, the pencil, or the graver.

We will confine our observation for a moment to the more mechanical work of the engraver as an example of simple attention. He sits with his eye and mind intent upon the fine lines of his copper or steel plate; and, as he looks more earnestly he holds his breath; and as his attention strengthens in its fixedness, his breathing becomes audible and irregular. Now and then he is forced to sigh to relieve his burdened and excited heart; for the blood is retarded in the lungs and brain, and if they be not soon relieved by some change of object or of action he turns faint and dizzy. Being wrought up to the same intensity day after day he comes at length upon the extreme verge of danger. The right ventricle of the heart becomes oppressed in consequence of imperfect action of the lungs, while the general circulation is quickened, and thus dilatation of the heart soon follows, with disordered liver and accumulation of black blood in the abdomen, bringing on a long train of morbid sensations, with constant dread of coming death. Moderate but frequent exercise in the open air, with cheerful society, as it would have prevented this miserable condition, will also still relieve it; but if this duty be neglected the

evil rapidly increases. The patient's heart palpi-
tates excessively when either the mind or the
body is hurried; he is " tremblingly alive" in every
limb, and his nervous system completely fails him.
Pallid, weak, timid and tremulous, he is apt to
become too sensitive to endure the anxieties of
domestic duty; and, if he be not sustained by
high religious or moral principles, he seeks a respite from his wretchedness in the soothing, yet
aggravating narcotism of opium or tobacco, or in
the insidious excitement of some fermented liquor;
and thus gradually casts himself out from all happy
and natural associations, and ends his days either
as a hypocondriac, a madman, or a drunkard.
This is not an exaggerated, but alas! a common
picture. The evil is aggravated in these cases by
the state of the mind, and that of the body being
equally irritable, they act and react on each other,
and the passions of the one, as well as the functions of the other, become so disordered that perfect sleep cannot be obtained, and the persistent
exhaustion produces a chronic fever, for which
rest, the only remedy, is sought in vain, except
in the grave.

The failure of the nervous system, and the fearful recourse to narcotics and stimulants for its relief, are often witnessed where the tyranny of
Mammon exacts too long an attention to the
mechanical and anxious business of art. Its re-

sults are still visible in a frightful degree amongst the operatives of our great manufactories, where the eye must be quick and the hand ever ready for one monotonous action, hour after hour and day after day, with the mathematical precision and rapidity of machinery, even through all that period of life when nature most demands a cheerful diversity of object and of action.

But the commercial Moloch demands the perpetual sacrifice of almost the whole bodily and mental being of those who are providentially so poor as to have nothing to sell but themselves. The millions sterling which their labours have won from many lands, belong to those who employ them; how then shall they be protected? Ceaseless toil is their protection, say some, because it preserves their morals! This subject however is too large for these pages. The great fact which we would observe, is, the power of his will over the body, for a man dies from voluntary fatigue, in the determination to employ his muscles. Whether he thus exhausts his vital energy in duty or for the indulgence of his appetites, he still demonstrates the dominance of his will, since he undergoes the extremity of toil to answer his own purpose, under whatever circumstances he may be constrained to exert himself. The will then is the master principle, even in a slave, and therefore its moral state must determine every man's moral destiny.

K

CHAPTER II.

If the nervous system allowed the mind to attend, reason would appear in its power as much at six years of age as at sixty. The child does reason then, and that correctly, to the extent of its knowledge; and is as capable of enjoying intellectual truth as in maturer years, provided the faculties be cultivated in an appropriate manner. Perhaps the most beautiful instance of such premature enjoyment is that furnished by Washington Irving, in his memoir of Margaret Davidson, a child, of whom it is stated that, when only in her sixth year, her language was elevated and her mind so filled with poetic imagery and religious thought, that she read with enthusiasm and elegance Thomson's Seasons, The Pleasures of Hope, Cowper's Task, and the writings of Milton, Byron, and Scott. The sacred writings were her daily study; and notwithstanding her poetic temperament, she had a high relish for history, and read with as much interest an abstruse treatise, that called forth the reflective powers, as she did poetry or works of imagination. Her physical frame was delicately constituted to receive impressions, and her mother was capable of observing and improving the opportunity afforded to instruct her. Nothing was learned by rote, and every object of her thought was discussed in conversation with a mind sympathizing with her own. Such a course, however, while it demonstrates the power of the mind, proves also that such premature employment of it is inconsistent with the physiology of the body; for while the spirit revelled in the ecstacies of intellectual excitement, the vital functions of the physical frame-work were fatally disturbed. She read, she wrote, she danced, she sung, and was the happiest of the happy; but, while the soul thus triumphed, the body became more and more delicate, and speedily failed altogether under the successive transports.

The brain of a child, however forward, is totally unfit for that intellectual exertion to which many fond parents either force or excite it. Fatal disease is thus frequently induced; and where death does not follow, idiocy, or at least such confusion of faculty ensues, that the moral perception is obscured, and the sensitive child becomes a man of hardened vice, or of insane self-will. Many examples of this may be found, particularly among the rigid observers of formal imitations of religion and the refined ceremonies of high civilization. There are numerous manuals to lead the infant mind from nature up to nature's God, as if it were in the nature of childhood to need manuals and catechisms of Botany, Geometry, and Astronomy to teach them the goodness of the Creator and the Saviour. Fathers and mothers rather need manuals to teach them how to treat their children, seeing that nearly half of those brought forth die in infancy, and the majority of the survivors are morbid both in mind and body. It is the parental character, in wisdom and love watching to bring the child into sympathy with true knowledge and affection, that represents and imitates the Divine Mind, as commended to our study by his acts. Even the persuasives of religious discipline, instead of falling like the gentle dew from heaven, are too frequently made hard and dry and harsh, as if the Gospel were the invention of a mathematical tyrant, to fashion souls by geometric rules, and not the expression of the mind of love, inspiring by example. The contrast, in personal appearance and manner, between a child trained under the winning management of a wise, firm, commanding love, and another subjected to the despotic control of fear is very striking.* In the former, we observe a spritely eye and open countenance, with a genial vivacity and trustfulness in the general expression of the body; a mixture of confiding sociality with intelligence, an alacrity of movement, and a healthiness of soul, evinced in generous activity and smiles. Even if the body be enfeebled, still a certain bright halo surrounds, as it were, the mental constitution. But physical, as well as intellectual vigour and enjoyment, are usually the happy result of that freedom of heart and generosity of spirit which skilful affection endeavours to encourage. Then, in youth and manhood, a noble intelligence confirming the propriety of such early training; but the child who finds a tyrant instead of a fostering parent, if naturally delicate, acquires a timid bearing, a languid gait, a sallow cheek, a pouting lip, a stupid torpidity, or a sullen defiance; for nature's defence from tyranny is either hard stupidity or cunning daring.

In this country the feeble slave too often skulks through life a cowering and cowardly hypocrite; defending himself from the craft and violence of others selfishness by every meanness, and seeking his enjoyment by the sly, as if he feared to be found susceptible of pleasure. His character is engraven on his face. The child of robust frame will however learn to face the tyrant, and, acquiring his worse features, at length be fit only to associate with ruffians, or to drive slaves.

Children are not formed for monotony and fixedness: their nervous systems will not bear it with impunity, and even their very bones are intolerant of the erect position for any length of time. They are made to be restless and active, and are not healthy if forced to be otherwise. The system of excessive restraint is therefore unchristian, because it is unnatural; for Christianity is not opposed to nature; it is not a violence, but a superior influence in correspondence with an inferior. It is a spirit that subdues by possessing the will, and which educates by inducing and fostering the sweet sympathies of religious love,— like the gentle dew, and the light and warmth of heaven, evolving the living seed. The government of fear and force is the plan of every imaginable hell, where each evil begets a greater, and terror and hatred torment each other. If then we would know how to manage a little child, let us imagine how Jesus would have treated it. Would he not have engaged its happiest feelings, and affections, won its heart, and blessed it? While sitting on his knee, would not the child have gazed into that "human face divine," and learned the gentleness and power of its Heavenly Father? Let it not be forgotten that the Saviour said, "whoso shall receive one such little child in my name, receiveth me: but whoso shall offend one of these little ones that believeth in me, it were better that a millstone were hanged about his neck and he drowned in the depth of the sea." If the words from which we obtain the notion do not deceive us, superior and holy beings are concerned about our offspring, and each child has its guardian angel, who beholds the face of God. How would that angel, if conversing with it, in visible beauty, talk to the child and kindle its affections? Surely by showing the might of graciousness with sublime simplicity; like that of the disciple whom Jesus loved, when he said, "little children, love one another." That angel would be more successful in his teaching only, because he would be more accommodating to the body, more earnest, more gentle, more attractive, and more sympathizing. He would have no greater truths to inculcate than we have, but knowing more clearly than we do the delicacy of our mysterious constitution and the worth of a soul, with its intellect and affections formed for eternity, he would act more gently and cautiously with its bodily temperament. Let us imitate the loving angel—the loving Saviour—the loving God —in kindness towards little children, and show them nothing but love; since they will respond to that spirit, but be repulsed into sin and agony by every other.

Piety itself is not unfrequently rendered terrible by a perverted application of memory, to descriptions in which Omnipotence is associated with the final judgment and the terrors of guilt. Many a little child, whose susceptible heart is as ready to yield to the gentlest breath of affection as the aspen-leaf to the zephyr, and whose spirit sparkles with love as readily as a dew-drop with the light, acquires the habit of terror, and scarcely dares to look up because he is taught as soon as he can speak to repeat—

> " There's not a sin that we commit,
>   Nor wicked word we say,
>   But in the dreadful book 'tis writ,
>   Against the judgment day."

And the thoughtless and fond parent too frequently makes that appear to be wickedness and sin which, however proper to childhood, is inconvenient to those who should tenderly train it. Surely that is a dangerous expedient for the correction of a child, conscious of having offended the only being he has learned to love, and while perhaps in agony of heart begging pardon from a mother, to be told to remember

> " There is a dreadful hell
>   And everlasting pains,
>   Where sinners must for ever dwell
>   In darkness, fire, and chains—
>
> " And can a wretch as I
>   Escape this cursed end, &c. ?"
>   *Divine Songs for Children.*

There is reason to believe that insane despondency and a disposition to suicide, may often be traced to abuse of religious discipline, if religious it may be called, especially that form of it just alluded to. Thus the impression of despair is apt to be burnt into the very brain, to "grow with its growth, and strengthen with its strength;" so that in after-life the divine remedy scarcely effaces the callous scar, or else the youth thus ill-treated in his childhood, endeavours to escape from the haunting terror by persuading himself that religion is invented only to keep wretches in order. Hence the glowing and glorious words of the living oracle—"There is joy amongst the angels in the presence of God over one sinner that repenteth"—is regarded only as an exquisite hyperbole. It falls dead upon the ear, as if it could not be, as it is, quickening truth from the lips of Him who is the Life.

There is another abuse here demanding remark. No treatment can be more injudicious and injurious than that often resorted to, even in schools of high character, namely, the exertion of memory, not for the sake of acquiring and retaining a knowledge of facts, which must always be useful, but merely to punish some dereliction. What good can arise from thus fatiguing the brain, by excessively straining that faculty, in the happy and spontaneous associations of which all the value of every acquirement consists? No plan is more likely to disable the mind and impair the body, as the servant of mind; for by this practice the idea of fixing the attention on words becomes peculiarly irksome. The very countenance of a boy thus distressed is apt to assume an expression of vacancy or irritability, and every function of his life to indicate the mischief arising from a debilitated brain under disorderly associations.

As the emulative success of classical education is generally dependent on an excessive determination of mind, for the purpose of rapidly loading the memory, it is of course attended for the most part with a correspondent risk to the nervous system of aspirants after academic honours. Mentally speaking, those who bear the palm in severe universities, rarely survive the effort necessary to secure the distinction. Like phosphorescent insects, their brilliance lasts but a little while, and is at its height when on the point of being extinguished for ever. The laurel crown is commonly for the dead; if not corporeally, yet spiritually; and those who attain the highest honours of their *Almæ Matres* are generally diseased men. Having reached the object of their aim, by concentrating their energies in one object, an intellectual palsy too often succeeds, and their bodies partake of the trembling feebleness. If their ambition survive, and instead of slumbering away a dreaming existence in some retired nook, they occupy prominent stations in public life, disease of the brain, heart or lungs soon quenches their glory, and they fade away. The impression of undue determination remains upon the brain, which continues subservient to the ambitious will until its structure and its functions fail together. The early effort opened a fountain of energy abruptly. It cannot be perennial; the waste is more rapid than the supply; and, like water bursting from its channel, it must run to waste, until violence ends in exhaustion. It happens, too, that those sanguine spirits, who acquire knowledge with facility and scatter it in wit, are rather the despisers of solid diligence; and therefore the great readers are mostly heavy-brained men, who make up in dogged determination and perseverance for lack of readiness in acquiring. With patience, equal to their ambition, they plod on for the prize. If they win it, their deadly passion is confirmed; if they lose it, again they roll the stone against the hill and it returns to crush them. Yet who would depreciate mental effort? The memory must be trained, the soul must be determined to conquer its impediments, the moral being will starve without a store of facts, the faculty of recollecting and arranging must be powerfully and regularly employed, or the mind becomes a desultory vagrant. Without mental exertion in acquiring habits of thought, youth would pass into manhood with the medley intellect and ungovernable nervous system of the savage, with all the corresponding disorderly habits of bodily action. Education distinguishes the energetic citizen from the fitful barbarian; the man who governs his body from the man who obeys it; the man of principles from the man of impulses. But we ought not to forget that true healthy education consists in the motives which naturally and quietly educe or lead out the mind to think for itself, in sympathy with those who have thought, not in the routine of school-tasks and verbal drudgery.

Intellectually speaking, man is not gregarious, but every mind has a track of its own as well as a body of its own; therefore, those who have felt the value of mental culture, and have taken their course untrammelled by task-work, have generally shown their intellectual vigour by a greater capacity of endurance as well as by freedom, boldness, and healthiness of thought. We may as well look for easy walking in a Chinese lady, whose feet have grown in iron shoes, and those very small ones, as for easy thinking in a mind that has been cast in a mould constructed to suit the minimi of the million. The reflective and perceptive faculties are too generally sacrificed at school for the sake of mere verbal memory; and hence those who were really most highly endowed, appeared, while there, most deficient scholars; such as Liebig, Newton, and Walter Scott.

In conclusion of this chapter we may observe, that the modern system of education appears to

be altogether unchristian; undoubtedly it contributes much to swell the fearful list of diseases,
for it is founded on an unhealthy emulation, which
ruins many both in body and in soul, while it
qualifies none the better either for business knowledge, usefulness, or enjoyment; but rather, together with the influence of the money valuation
of intellect, causes the most heroic spirits of our
age to hang upon vulgar opinion and the state of
the market.

CHAPTER III.

PECULIAR EFFECTS OF INORDINATE MENTAL DETERMINATION.

THE strongest brain will fail under the continuance of intense thought. All persons, who have been accustomed to close study, will remember the utter and indescribable confusion that comes over the mind when the will has wearied the brain. A curious example has already been given in the case of Spalding, who tells us that his attention having been long kept on the stretch, and also greatly distracted, he was called upon to write a receipt, but he had no sooner written two words than he could proceed no further. For half an hour he could neither think consecutively nor speak except in words which he did not intend. Afterwards he recovered, and found that instead of writing on the receipt " fifty dollars, being half a year's rate, &c.," he had written " fifty dollars, through the salvation of Bra—," the last word being left unfinished, and without his having the least recollection of what he intended it to be. This state presents a specimen of partial delirium or waking dream: the will still acting, but incapable of controlling the thoughts or connecting memory with present impression. This must depend on the state of nerve produced by the mental intensity, which, when continued to extreme exhaustion, we know to be capable of so altering the sensation as that objects presented to the eye assume appearances which do not belong to them. Thus Sir Joshua Reynolds, after being occupied for many hours in painting, saw trees in lamp posts, and moving shrubs in men and women. This kind of inability to command attention is most readily induced by monotonous study. Persons of lymphatic temperament are peculiarly liable to this kind of exhaustion, and should therefore employ their minds with great caution, or otherwise their determination will prove the destruction of their reason; for, in fact, a persistance of this want of control over attention is insanity, as we see in those instances in which persons confound things together of an incongruous nature; as when the anatomist, having fatigued his nervous system by a long continued dissection, talked of a town to which he referred as situated in the deltoid muscle. Disorder from excessive attention is sometimes manifested in a still odder manner, as in the case of the celebrated Dr. Watts, who, after great exertion of mind, thought his head too large to allow him to pass out at the study door. A gentleman, after delivering a lecture at the College of Surgeons, said that

his head felt as if it filled the room.   Sometimes
fatigue produces permanent insanity.   Thus, in
the German Psychological Magazine, a case is
related of a soldier who, after great fatigue, happened to read the book of Daniel, and from that
moment believed that he could perform miracles,
such as plant an apple-tree which, by his power,
should bear cherries.   Determinate effort of mind
sometimes induces a peculiar insanity, when the
nervous system becomes habituated to extreme
exhaustion.   A certain form of this malady occurs
in paroxysms of ecstatic abstraction suddenly seizing the person and fixing him like a living statue;
with the body slightly bent, every limb rigid with
rapture, the arms elevated, the fore-finger pointed
to some imagined object, the eyelids staring wide,
the eyes turned up with an intense and motionless expression, and the lips a little separated; in
short, the whole attitude and countenance expressive of the most awful admiration.   This is
the description of a real case arising from intense
concentration of thought, continued without regard to bodily exercise or proper change in the
mental object.

It is remarkable that similar states may be
produced by the will of another, even in those
who have not shown any tendency to it, when
they surrender their wills to the impressions produced by another's action.   Baron Dupotet, who

MENTAL DETERMINATION.   209

lately made some noise in London by his feats of mesmerism, had the power, by his manœuvres, of speedily throwing certain individuals either into sleep, or convulsions, or a rigid condition, such as that just described. This was effected without any collusion, and in many cases without the slightest idea on the patient's part of what was likely to follow. Such facts are never disputed by physiologists now, and perhaps they may be generally accounted for by the direct action of the mind on the body, or at least by mental excitement in connexion with some disorder of the nervous system; since they are quite in keeping with what we observe to arise independently of those tricks of hand called animal magnetism. In these cases, as far as I have witnessed them, there appears to be a propagation of impression from the senses, especially sight, to the centre of the individual's nervous system, thereby altering the direction of nervous energy. Intense and eager attention, with undefined dread, and with the eye fixed on the hand or eye of a person apparently set upon bewitching one, is a process which few could submit to for any length of time without strange sensations being produced. Hence it has happened that a firm man, who knew nothing about the matter, has sat down with laughter, but soon his attention has been fixed upon the wizard's hand, and ere long he has looked unutterably

stupid, like a drunkard, then turned pale, then
become immoveable, except just as the magician
before him was pleased to point—now with his
nose to the ground—now upwards—now aslant—
now with body twisted this way—now that—now
standing—now sitting—and now walking, or rather
stalking, just at the pantomimic indications of the
enchanter; and all this, as it appeared, simply
from the effect of an unnatural and overpowering
attention on a brain unprepared by a habit of
healthy action.

In ecstasy or trance, the patient's mind is absorbed on some object of imagination; as the
term ecstasy implies, persons so impressed are out
of the body, engrossed in spiritual contemplations.
The muscles are sometimes relaxed, at other times
rigid; the will, however, often continues to exert
an influence over certain parts of the body, such
as the organs of voice; for though they are incapable of moving a limb, or being excited by any
external stimulus, they nevertheless occasionally
give expression to their feelings by singing or
speaking. This kind of entrancing delirium is
apt to occur in persons afflicted by nervous disorder, especially where the will is wayward; and
may frequently be produced in them by powerful
excitement of the imagination, or by mesmeric
manipulations. It is stated by individuals well
qualified to detect imposition, that in these cases

there exists a kind of transference and concentration of intelligence in certain parts of the nervous system, so that a sort of oracular faculty is developed, and the subjects of this affection become capable of describing things beyond the range of their senses and of foretelling events. Dr. Copland states that many of the Italian improvvisatori possess their peculiar faculty only in this state of ecstacy, or, as it may be called, abnormal consciousness, from resolute attention to ideas.

Probably the mind and the nervous system are intensely excited for some time previous to the development of ecstacy. There is a morbid acuteness of feeling and thought, an inordinate employment of the attention, kept up by preceding sensations, or some absorbing train of ideas, which exhaust the sensorium, and bring it into that state in which it often appears to be in those persons who accustom themselves to abstract studies and reverie. This condition is more apt to occur when strong passions are associated with a weak body. A frequent and exhausting repetition of pleasureable feelings begets a marked predisposition to this disordered action of the brain.

If all that is stated concerning ecstacy be true, we are forced to the conclusion that, after the exhaustion of brain is carried to a certain extent, the mind begins voluntarily to exert itself in a new and enlarged manner, so as to exhibit phenomena which have been named lucidity, exaltation of faculty, clairvoyance, &c.   The transition state may present appearances like those of common delirium, dreaming, somnabulism, and madness. It is often accompanied by convulsions.   A few cases of an extraordinary kind may best illustrate this curious subject.   It has been testified that cataleptic patients often manifest a clairvoyant faculty.   A patient of Petetin, President of the Medical Society of Lyons, in this state, is said to have distinguished in succession several cards laid on her stomach under the bed-clothes; she told the hour of a watch held in the closed hand of an inquirer, and recognized a medal grasped in the hand of another; she read a letter placed under the waistcoat of her physician and mentioned the number of gold and silver coins contained in each end of a purse which had been slipped there by a sceptic.   She told each of the persons present what he possessed about him most remarkable, and perceived through a screen what one person was doing.

According to the testimony of the committee of the medical section of the French Royal Academy, a man named Paul, having been mesmerized, besides many other equally wonderful things, read a book opened at random while his eyes were forcibly closed by M. Jules Cloquet.   He had been mesmerized by M. Foissac.   The committee also bear evidence that other individuals in the same state could read distinctly and play at cards with the greatest dexterity and correctness. Their report also declares, "that in two somnambulists they found the faculty of foreseeing. One of them announced repeatedly several months previously, the day, the hour and the minute of the access and return of epileptic fits. The other announced the period of his cure. These previsions were realized with remarkable exactness."

Those who are curious in these marvels may find abundance of them in many modern works. It certainly would be passing strange should such relations all prove false, since the acutest observers of all ages have declared them to be true. At least Hippocrates, Aretæus, Aristotle, &c., describe with great minuteness, and in strict accordance with the statements of recent and competent believers, a state of the body in which the powers of the soul are exalted. Thus Hippocrates says, "there is a class of diseases in which men discourse with eloquence and wisdom, and predict secret and future events; and this they do though they are ignorant rustics and idiots." Aretæus states that the mind under certain circumstances of disease becomes clear and prophetic for some patients "predict their own end and certain events of interest to those around, who think them talking deliriously, but nevertheless are amazed to find their predictions true."

Alsaharavius says, he has known many epileptics who had a knowledge of things which he was sure they had never learned. The occasional prevision of the dying has been credited by almost every nation, and the faculty of second sight has been almost as universally acknowledged.

In most of the cases related in this chapter, it is probable that the attention was kept so long intensely fixed on one set of objects, that at length the brain took on a new action, as if from physiological necessity, or because the law of its organization demanded a change, violent in proportion to its abuse. We know that there is, while awake, a tendency to repeat sensations and ideas in an accustomed manner, and that there is also during the suspension of outward attention, a tendency to a state contrary to that previously existing; thus a man who has been almost maddened by vain desire, say for food, will, during his sleep, enjoy a fancied feast. From this and many similar facts we learn that the mind possesses the power of securing its own satisfaction when withdrawn from the demands of the body; that one train of ideas can be displaced only by substituting another; that obedience to the laws of our bodily and mental economy is imperative; and hence that there is a necessity for exercising the will in a judicious, moral and religious manner, if we would enjoy a healthy habit of thinking and acting.

CHAPTER IV.

THE EFFECTS OF UNDUE ATTENTION TO ONE'S OWN BODY.

It has been already observed, that the education of the senses is a mental act, in which attention and comparison are busily at work, to determine the relation of objects to each other and to the individual regarding them. Where the organs are perfect, the power of perception or the acuteness of sensation is in proportion to the power of the mind in directing attention, or in proportion to the degree in which the particular sense is used, hence we find microscopic observers, for instance, acquire such a command over their sight, in the use of their instruments, as to detect the minutest variations in objects and such slight shades of difference as would be altogether overlooked by persons unaccustomed to such investigations. This education of sense, under the tuition of the will, is displayed in the most remarkable manner among those savage tribes, whose very existence depends upon the keenness of their senses, in discovering indications of danger or of safety among the wilds in which they dwell, and where civilized men would be wholly at a loss either to track prey or to avoid an enemy. The dominion of the mind over certain organs of the body is beautifully shown in such instances; but there are curious facts in connexion with this subject well worthy of observation. It is not the senses merely that may be rendered more acute by effort of mind. Attention to any part of the body is capable of exalting the sensibility of that part or of causing the consciousness concerning its state to be affected in a new manner. Thus a man may attend to his stomach till he feels the process of digestion; to his heart, till conscious of its contractions; to his brain, till he turns dizzy with a sense of action within it; to any of his limbs, till they tingle; to himself, till tremblingly alive all over; and to his ideas till he confounds them with realities.

We have remarked that persons of high intellectual endowment are capable of abstracting the attention from external objects, and of so applying it to the objects of thought as to become almost insensible to those of sense. On this power of abstraction depends the degree and success of studious habit. By it reason expands the scope of her vision, and acquires increased sagacity in every fresh exercise of her faculties. Fixing the attention on abstract truths is like lifting the veil between the world of sense and the world of spirit.* By endeavouring to look, we see further

along the vista of life, and by abstraction we place
ourselves in a position to be actuated by new
influences. By striving and urging after truth,
we get more and more familiar with her footsteps.
When we would learn more of some mystery
important to us, we turn away from all other
subjects, and cast our attention in upon the consciousness of our own spirits, as if expecting there
to discover a reply to our inquiry; and by thus
standing, as it were, in the attitude of expectation, to observe thoughts as they pass before us,
we often discover great secrets, and find our moral
nature enlightened and enlarged by new convictions and new desires; for by this mental retirement we become most susceptible of spiritual impressions. But, by some mysterious re-action,
this strong awakening of the mind renders it
more conscious of the body, when the abstraction
is over, and hence the most intellectual are
generally also the most sensitive of mortals.

Many diseases are produced, increased, and
perpetuated by the attention being directed to the
disordered part; but employment, which diverts
the attention from disease, often cures it. Every
one who has had a tooth drawn, knows the charm
of expecting the final agony;—a sight of the
operator or the instruments has put the pain to
flight. The celebrated metaphysician, Kant, was
able to forget the pain of gout by a voluntary

L

effort of thought, but it always caused a dangerous rush of blood to the head.

We may compare sensibility to a fluid, as
Cabanis did, and suppose it to exist in a determinate quantity, capable of being diverted from
one channel into another, according to the state
of the mind and nervous system ; thus causing an
accumulation of exalted sensibility in one part
of the body and a proportionate diminution in
other parts.   This state existed in the cases cited
in a former chapter.   In ecstacies the brain and
sympathetic nerves appear to become highly energetic, while the vital feeling seems to have forsaken
other parts of the system.   Something akin to
this must have taken place in those violent
fanatics, the Convulsionists of St. Medard, who
submitted with impunity and pleasure to severe
wounds from swords and hatchets, which, in the
ordinary state of sensibility, would have destroyed
life.   But these ecstatic and ascetic beings called
such blows their consolations, and entreated to be
mangled and beaten by the strongest men and
the largest weapons.

The mesmeric magic also, by giving a strong
and new determination to the mind, seems to
endow it with new power of action, by calling into
exercise a concentrated or intense sensibility, and
a mode of nervous energy to which the organs
have not been accustomed, and which therefore

induces an apparently supernatural train of phenomena; for function and orgasm seem to be due
to the unknown agent which confers sensibility
and action upon structure.

The attention being unduly fixed upon the body
itself, instead of being employed in controlling
the limbs and senses in active exercise about the
proper business of life, causes, or at least often ag-
gravates, the morbid consciousness which torments
the hypochondriac. The sensation of disease of
course may precede this, and is perhaps necessary
to the first excitement of attention to the vital
functions in an unnaturally acute manner, but
perverted consciousness commences the instant
we fail to obey the laws of our constitution, which
require us to attend to other objects rather than
to ourselves. If we use not our faculties on their
proper objects, improper thoughts will present
themselves, and the moral equilibrium will thus
be destroyed by inward and selfish attention, and
the intellectual eye-sight become confirmed in its
obliquity; for we are intended to be healthy and
happy only as long as our minds are occupied in
acquiring intelligence from things around us, or
by reciprocal interest with other beings. It would
indeed appear that our Creator designed us to be
employed rather on objects around us, and in
association with the activities of other minds, than
on the operations of our own; for we find that

our efforts to concentrate attention on the process of our own thoughts speedily begets a most
painful confusion ; nor can we even summon
our memory for the restoration of a forgotten idea
and search with any diligence for its recovery,
without such fatigue as either compels us soon to
relinquish the pursuit, or else, if we obstinately
persist, induces a nervous headache and imbecility, nearly approaching to aberration of intellect.   The mastery over our own minds, except
in obedience to social laws, is denied to us.
Healthy thinking and mental association are one.
If we would think safely we must think naturally;
that is, in relation to others, and our thoughts
must lead to action.   There must be a degree of
spontaneous readiness and submission of mind to
the common course of association and feeling.
Not that we possess no power of selecting from
the ideas which present themselves to our imagination.   Far otherwise—the gift and extent of
reason consists in this selection ; but the success
with which we employ our faculties depends not
on desire but on training, that is, on the habit of
our intellect in sympathy with other minds, and
according to our familiarity with facts, appearances and employments.   In short, observation is
the basis of our ability, and outward exertion is
its security ; but self-consciousness, or attentive
analysis of the operations and sensations of our

own minds, endangers the well-being of our reason, and is the frequent cause of insanity. Hence,
then, we learn the paramount importance of our
sympathies being suitably excited, for this is
proper mental cultivation.

To this end it is essential that the growing mind
should be educated in truth under the direction
of those who themselves feel and obey it. The
will of one is influenced by the will of others, and
the union of a body of persons, under the same
proper convictions, is, especially to youthful reason and affection, the strongest safeguard and
most persuasive government. Hence the value
of some central truth attracting together individuals, who will test all their opinions by their one
uniting faith. Christianity is founded on this
principle; for it is a central light which imparts
due colour to all objects, and it is evermore successful in proportion as its one grand truth is insisted on and believed.

The sanity of society, as well as of individual
minds, is secured only by faith in some common
object of regard, and the commencement both of
personal and social hypocrisy is the abstraction of
regard from the common interest, for the purpose
of attending to self. Here schism and confusion
begin, but here they do not end; for party spirit, or
endemic hypocrisy, is but extended selfishness, and
personal moral derangement made more general

and infectious. We see then that obedience alone
is safety; but the idea of obedience implies a
belief in the revelation of a supreme will; a power
regarding which we cannot dispute; for as long
as we question the existence of supreme power
and appointment, we deny the right to govern,
even in the Almighty. It follows, then, that in
order to the formation of true moral impressions,
correct thinking, and hence correct conduct, there
must be a true revelation of God's will. The
legitimate end of this argument then appears to
be, that if God has revealed himself, as we believe
He has in nature, naturally, in the Bible, ex-
plicitly, then our business with regard to both
revelations is to learn and to obey, since nothing
more is needed for our happiness. In fact our
faculties are fit for nothing else, and if we insist
upon employing them in any other manner we
must meet the penalty,—madness and misery.

> ——— ——— " All declare
> For what the Eternal Maker has ordained
> The powers of man : we feel within ourselves
> His energy divine : he tells the heart
> He meant, he made us to behold and love
> What he beholds and loves, the general orb
> Of life and being—to be great like him,
> Beneficent and active."—*Akenside.*

But to return to the effect of attention on the
body. There is an artificial mode of producing

sleep, by fatiguing the muscles of the eye, which is effected by a strained and intent gaze at any object, real or ideal, viewed under an acute angle. Perhaps by this effort the irritability of those muscles becomes exhausted and also that of the optic nerve—the result is giddiness, mistiness of sight and soon after sleep. Congestion is induced in the eyes, and carried thence to the optic and other nerves of the eyes, and owing to their proximity to the origin of the nerves of respiration and circulation, sympathetically affects these also, and thus enfeebles the action of the heart and lungs. If the mind resign itself to sleep, an orderly slow breathing takes place, and the whole body soon becomes composed ; but if mental effort continue to resist the disposition to drowsiness, another order of phenomena occurs, similar to those frequently arising from mesmerism. The heart's more feeble action first produces coldness of the extremities and general pallor of the surface; the blood is consequently accumulated in the region of the heart. The brain, and probably the spinal and sympathetic system of nerves, become congested in consequence, and then many strange and curious phenomena, resulting from irregularity in the circulation of the blood and nervous energy, spedily follow. The inability to raise the upper eyelid under these circumstances arises from a kind of paralysis of its muscles; a paralysis which is apt at the same time to affect other parts. Of course morbid consciousness, in various organs of the body, is manifested according to the different modifications of mental and bodily constitution in the various persons subjected to such experiments.

A case is related by Dr. George Cheyne, which affords a very curious illustration of the voluntary influence of the mind over the body in modifying vital action and sensibility. A Colonel Townsend, residing at Bath, sent for Drs. Baynard and Cheyne and a Mr. Skrine, to give them some account of an odd sensation which he had for some time felt, which was, that he could expire when he pleased, and, by an effort, come to life again. He insisted so much on their seeing the trial made that they were forced at last to comply. They all three felt his pulse which was distinct, and had the usual beat. He then composed himself on his back for some time. By the nicest scrutiny they were soon unable to discover the least sign of life, and at last were satisfied that he was actually dead; and were just about to leave him, with the idea that the experiment had been carried too far, when they observed a slight motion in the body, and gradually the pulsation of the heart returned, and he quite recovered. In the evening of the same day, however, he composed himself in the same manner and really died. Disease of the heart, under unnatural attention to the organ, caused the phenomena. Cardan must have been subject to some singular disease, for he says, " Whenever I wish it, I can go out of my body so as to feel no sensation whatever; as if I were in ecstacy. When I enter this state, or more properly speaking, when I plunge myself into ecstacy, I feel my soul issuing out of my heart, and as it were quitting it, as well as the rest of my body, through a small aperture formed at first in the head and particularly in the cerebellum. This aperture, which runs down the spinal column, can only be kept open by great effort. In this situation I feel nothing but the bare consciousness of existing out of my own body, from which I am distinctly separated. But I cannot remain in this state more than a very few moments."

Some strange philosophers have entertained so daring an idea of the mightiness of the will over the vital organization as to declare that if a man determined not to die he would not. The will, however, has scarcely anything to do with the matter; for it is a fact that the bodily condition immediately preceding death generally produces, or at least is accompanied by such a quiescence of mind, that volition itself seems to slumber or consent to death, and there is almost always after long and great debility a peaceful anticipation of the coming event.

CHAPTER V.

MISEMPLOYMENT OF THE MIND.

THE foregoing facts forcibly teach us, as indeed does every man's experience, that rest is as necessary as action, and neither body nor mind continue fit for the business of this life without an occasional withdrawal of the will, either in sleep, or in a little quiet castle-building, or brown study.

> " The understanding takes repose
> In indolent vacuity of thought,
> And sleeps and is refreshed."

The mind thus proceeds dreamily, and therefore without that determination of blood to the brain which the continued exercise of volition and desire always occasions; for the will demands a large supply of blood in order to evolve nervous power for the energizing of the muscles, as volition is peculiarly associated with muscular function, proving that healthy will is necessarily connected with bodily activity. This indolent vacuity, however, may become habitual, and then a legion of evils of the worse kind crowd in upon the soul, for irritability takes the place of natural action when the body is not duly employed.

Neglect of education often causes permanent inability to maintain attention. If the faculties be not strengthened by occasional exercise under proper teaching, the soul becomes at length the slave of imagination, and is apt to dally with any empty fancy that may attract it. Some *ignis fatuus*, some foolish glitter of false light, is the only object likely to be pursued by a person who has not been taught from childhood the use of reason, or who has not enjoyed the blessing of high motives and encouragement imparted by example. If such a one read, it is for amusement, without the smallest power of grasping argument; and he being, from the idle habit of the brain, at the mercy of vulgar or ludicrous associations, the most serious subjects provoke loose ideas, instead of conducing to thoughtfulness and improvement. This kind of madness is very common with ill-educated young persons, before the trials of life correct their vagrant fancies, and subdue their selfishness. Frivolity of mind sometimes settles into permanent insanity in such persons, and a multiplicity of unmeaning, unprofitable, unapplied thoughts succeed each other with ungoverned rapidity; for imagination must act when the will and judgment decline their duty; and thus at length the poor imbecile trifler, by the abuse of his nervous system, has his life converted into a miserable dream, and he becomes visibly a fool;

for his form and features, action and expression, correspond with his mental imbecility. The
pursuit of sensual exciting and enervating pleasures,—another turn which the mind not intellectually employed is apt to take,—speedily conducts
the giddy youth, as many such cases testify, to
the worst cells of the madhouse. The stock of
enjoyment being soon exhausted, the brain becomes useless; and worn in body and debased in
mind, the wretched victim of imaginative sensuality is early subjected to every species of morbid sensation and desire. Having neither taste
nor energy for rational pursuit, without resource
in intellect, affection or religion, he becomes at
length the prey of a terrible despair, which terminates only in idiocy or death.

Sentimentalism, and all other mental extrava-
gancies, are but the different directions which
uncultivated minds are accustomed to take, and
unhappily these dispositions are highly contagious.
"There is nothing so absurd, false, prodigious,
but either out of affection of novelty, simplicity,
blind zeal, hope and fear, the giddy-headed multitude will embrace it, and without examination
approve it."* All these are evinced by bodily
peculiarities and disorders in keeping with their
mental causes, and thus men's creeds and fancies
are almost expressed in their bodies. The conta-

* Burton.

gion of folly, moreover, spreads widely and rapidly;
because the physical constitution of fallen man is
in direct sympathy with those passions which
most readily manifest themselves in the features,
the attitude, the action, the language, the tone
of voice, the turn of a hand. We are all more
or less moved by what we witness of feeling in
others; and as, when the body is weakened by
fatigue, nervous disorders—such as hysteria, convulsions, and epilepsy—may be communicated to
multitudes by their compliance with the instinct
of imitation; so the powerful exhibition of any
passion or enthusiasm is apt to impress all those
who witness it with a potency, proportioned to
the vigour of their nerves and the degree of control which their reason is accustomed to exercise
over their sensations. We may thus readily account for the wide and almost universal diffusion
of the dancing mania, and other maladies, partaking both of a moral and a physical character,
during the dark ages and amongst people unblest
by the restraining habits and elevating associations
of rational and religious education. All history is
full of evidence that ignorant minds yield at once
to the force of sensual impressions; and that,
because the brain and nerves, when not governed
by indwelling intelligence, are predisposed to obey
whatever impulse from without may demand their
sympathy. Hence also every species of violent

emotion is irresistibly propagated amongst such persons; for insanity, and the most obstinate forms of nervous disorder, thus become epidemic; and, like the swine possessed by the legion of demons, those who are not fortified by truth rush one after another over the precipice to destruction. When considering the influence of sympathy, we shall find further illustrations of this subject. But not only are such thoughtless ill-trained persons apt to suffer in this manner, but also all who live rather in lonely speculation than in active usefulness. Such individuals are exceedingly liable to a disorder called hypochondriasis, which is manifestly connected with bodily disease, arising from injudicious employment of the brain, in solitary musings and deep and protracted study, or anxieties without the relief of frequent social intercourse and cheerful exercise. Luther, speaking of his own tendency to this malady, arising from excessive and anxious application, says, " Heavy thoughts do enforce rheums: when the soul is busied with grievous cogitations, the body must partake of the same. When cares, heavy cogitations, sorrows and passions, do exceed, then they weaken the body; which, without the soul, is dead, or like a horse without one to rule it. But when the heart is at rest and quiet, then it taketh care of the body. Whoso is possessed with these trials, should in no case be alone nor hide himself, and so bite and torment himself with his and the devil's cogitations and possessings; for the Holy Ghost saith, 'Woe to him that is alone.'"

Of course as the mind is always employed while a person is awake, one train of ideas cannot be displaced but by substituting another. Hence the importance of change of place and of object when the affections or emotions are morbidly excited, or the nervous system enervated by the continued action of one train of thought.

Hypochondriasis presents itself in the most whimsical forms, in consequence of the morbid condition of those nerves which conduce to sensation. Thus some imagine themselves dead, and others declare their bodies to be the abode of unheard-of maladies. One thinks his stomach is full of frogs, and he hears them croak; another thinks his body a lump of butter, and he is afraid to walk in the sun lest he should be melted. A lady, who had led an idle life, imagined herself a pound of candles, and dreaded the approach of night, fearing the maid should take a part of her for use.

That illusive convictions are all more or less associated with actual disorder of that part of the nervous system on which perception depends, is evident from sensation being so blunted in many bad cases, that persons so afflicted do not feel anything applied to the skin. This is exemplified to the greatest extent in a case related by Foville. A man was wounded at the battle of Austerlitz, and ever after he was insanely convinced that he had no bodily existence; and there seemed to be no method of convincing him to the contrary, for in fact he was not sensible of anything done to his body unless he saw the action: feeling was quite absent. Whether this affection arose from impression first received on his mind, or on his body, it is difficult to discover; but it is certain that such maladies are sometimes cured by merely convincing the mind of its mistake.

Nervous diseases, being disorders of sensation as well as of will, are to be treated with great patience and forbearance; although the whimsicalities of the complaint are frequently so ludicrous that "to be grave exceeds all power of face." Many droll stories might be written concerning them, but who can deem them fit to be laughed at? It will be found that nervous exhaustion, from over attention, or repeated sensation without proper intervals of rest, is the common cause of this strange malady. These states of mind may perhaps be sometimes the result of violent, long-continued, and irresistible emotion; yet we must not be unmindful that they are frequently the inevitable consequence of neglecting the early discipline of the will; for the dominion of passion over judgment generally presupposes a moral dereliction.

The potency of emotion over our bodies is every where visible; for our whole active life is altogether an exhibition of passions at their work, and our projects and our plans are directed to no other end than the gratification of desire. The most restless spirit soonest destroys the body, but the most bustling is not the busiest soul—mental intensity is silent. It is the mind that uses life, and the law of our earthly existence is equally broken both by inaction and by excess. The motive power requires regulation; for whether too rapid or too slow, if the action be irregular, the machinery is equally endangered. We are formed for moderation; and our safety consists only with the steady employment of vital power under moral restraints; hence distinctness of object and purpose is essential to health of mind, and for the preservation of that orderly action of the nervous system without which we are diseased in body also. Every faculty and function therefore requires its appropriate exercise, for inaction is scarcely more liable to be followed by a morbid train of miseries than is disappointed or distracted activity. The interruption of a mental purpose or desire involves the material through which the mind acts in its own disorder, as the machinery suffers when the

power which puts it into motion is fitfully employed, or unduly excited or misdirected.   Our
experience testifies that the greatest mental confusion and distress of brain arise not so much from
steadily continued and determined effort of the
mind, in a rational manner, as from interruption
to the purpose of the will.   Thus, when some
daily vexation breaks the chain of thought, or
draws the attention off from the intellectual pursuit on which the spirit had earnestly been bent,
displeasure and distraction take the place of com-
placency, and the cause of the disturbance is apt,
when thus frequently returning, to take complete
possession of the mind, and to haunt the attention
like a hateful goblin, blighting the soul with its
cloudy presence.   Hence the soured misanthrope
often appears when the philosopher might have
been expected; for unless the man of thought has
his heart soothed by affectionate and comfortable
appliances, in a suitable and seasonable manner,
his resolute and perplexed spirit, incapable of resting from reflection, is very likely to find successive
vexations terminate in madness, or some milder
form of mental derangement or unhappy eccen-
tricity, which constrains him to seek pleasure only
in imagination and with solitude.

Those who are connected with persons consti-
tutionally prone to reflectiveness cannot be too
cautious in their manner of opposing the bias of

their dispositions, or too gently endeavour to win them from the danger of absorbing study, for both their sensibilities and affections are generally fine in proportion to the intensity with which they habitually contemplate the objects of their attention.   Men of genius, whatever the direction of their minds, are usually as full of feeling as of thought, their intellect being urged on under the dominion of that love which cannot rest without constant approval.   Their habit of abstraction may cause them to appear selfish, unsocial, or absurdly whimsical, but they are only engaged too intensely to exhibit in an ordinary manner the appearance of passing interest.   They are, however, exactly those who are most subject to insanity, as their minds are kept unavoidably busy to the full extent of nervous endurance.   Yet persons of this deep style of thinking and feeling are most devoted to the well-being of others, and are the first to demonstrate the nobility of their nature by those self-sacrifices which have distinguished the best names in history.

Cowper and Byron may be instanced as opposite examples of bad modes of education, terminating in morbid habits of thinking, and exhibiting by fits and starts the finest traits of generous nature in the most contrary and inconsistent manners.

CHAPTER VI.

CHAGRIN AND SUICIDE.

WE know that determination must vastly excite the brain when the student or the statesman is induced by desire for doubtful distinction, to spend his days and his nights in the distractions of vacillating hopes and fears. Under the strain of these conflicting passions how many a mighty mind sinks into insanity amidst the mysterious darkness of which some demon whispers close upon the ear, "No hope, no aim, no use in life, the knife is now before you." Long, however, before this terrific state of mind occurs, the body gives unheeded warning of the growing danger, by irregular appetites, tormenting visions, and unaccountable sensations; for insanity is always a bodily malady, although perhaps in most cases moral delinquency is superadded, and the will has been disordered before the body. Although the destructive propensity may sometimes cause suicide under a sudden impulse, or it may even arise from a morbid disposition to imitate, yet it is probable that the irritability of the body, which

allows not a respite to the soul, from the constant
stimulus to attention and will, most frequently
drives the melancholy maniac to commit suicide.
Death seems in these cases the only refuge from
the weary vigilance of morbid sensibility. This
awful remedy is frequently sought under the impulse of a kind of instinct, when the mind becomes
so possessed by its misery as to be quite incapable
of comparing the desire felt with previous convictions, and so the patient is blindly urged on,
by longing for relief, to use the first opportunity
for self-destruction which may present itself,
association only serving to connect the means of
death with the idea of escape from a tormenting
body or some haunting impression. The frequent
connection of the disposition to suicide with the
despondent forms of insanity, warrants the sup-
position that despair, if not met by the solace of
affection, would always lead its subject to the same
dark resort; as the scorpion is said to destroy itself
with its own sting, when encircled by dangers from
which it cannot escape.

The love of approbation, which is closely connected with the love of society, is generally the
strongest of our passions, and is that by which the
lower passions are restrained within the limits of
common decorum. It is the disappointment of
this passion, or chagrin, which most frequently
disposes to suicide. Man's hell is the feeling of

solitude, or the dread of being despised; and if his associates cast him out of their pale, or appear completely to excommunicate him from their sympathies, he seems as if at once possessed by Satan. Should this wounding of his proud desire deprive him of all hope of restoration to the heart at least of some one being who can love him in spite of his faults, he will rush unbidden into the darkness of another world, the apprehension of which is less terrible to him than the loneliness in which he suffers. So common is this catastrophe, that it appears like the result of a natural law of the guilty mind, when unacquainted with divine truth, and unsustained by the hopeful consciousness of spiritual and eternal life. Hence heathenism and infidelity have always approved self-murder as the proper remedy of extreme vexation.

If we may credit report, it would appear that mere animals are also impelled by the same feeling under similar circumstances: thus it is related in the Travels and Adventures of Monsieur Violet, the truth of which is avouched by Captain Maryatt, that he saw horses, that had been tyrannized over by other horses, and treated by the whole herd as outcasts, commit suicide. When tired of their *paria* life they walk round and round some large tree, as if to ascertain the degree of hardness required, measure their distance, and darting with furious speed against it, fracture their skulls, and thus get rid of life and oppression together. He says that squirrels sometimes persecute one among their number till he destroys himself; and he states, that " one day while we were watching this outcast of a squirrel, we detected a young one slowly creeping through the adjoining shrubs, he had in his mouth a ripe fruit, at every moment he would stop and look if he were watched, just as if he feared detection. At last he arrived near the paria, or outcast, and deposited before him his offering to misery and old age. We watched this spectacle with feelings which I could not describe: there was such a show of meek gratitude on the one side and happiness on the other, just as if he enjoyed his good action. They were, however, perceived by the other squirrels, who sprang by dozens upon them; the young one with two bounds escaped, the other submitted to his fate. I rose. All the squirrels vanished except the victim; but that time, contrary to his habits, he left the shrub and slowly advanced to the bank of the river and ascended a tree. A minute afterwards we observed him at the very extremity of a branch projecting over the rapid waters, and we heard his plaintive shriek. It was his farewell to life and misery." This story will serve as a parable expressive of human conduct—but one amongst a multitude runs the risk of showing kindness to the outcast, while the rest are bent upon driving the wretched to destruction.

The association between neglect, ill-usage, despondency, and suicide, is of great practical importance, especially in relation to those who suffer from the terrors of that most awful malady, religious despair, which usually commences with seclusion, and a state the reverse of self-complacency, conjoined with strong affection insufficiently regarded.

Happy is it if the suicidal catastrophe be averted by such a failure of some organ or function of the body as shall arrest the ambitious, the wayward, or the lonely spirit even with the stroke of death; but more blessed still to find association with calm and loving minds, and, like Kirke White, to take admonishment from the uncertainty and comparative worthlessness of this world's honours and attachments, to prepare for the untiring activities of a nobler state.

" Come, Disappointment, come !
        Though from hope's summit hurled,
        Still rigid nurse thou art forgiven,
        For thou, severe, wert sent from heaven
            To wean me from the world ;
                To turn mine eye
                    From vanity,
        And point to scenes of life that never, never die."

This reference to Kirke White reminds us that

the influence of the mental state is remarkably
exhibited in the progress of organic diseases.
Medical practitioners can bear ample testimony
to the fact, that religious feeling, that is, calm
resignation to the supreme will, soothes and tran-
quillizes the sufferer's frame more than all medical
appliances. Often does he witness the triumph
of faith over bodily affliction, as consumption for
instance, with slow and fatal hand steals away the
life-blood from the youth who lately, perhaps in
the height of moral danger, adorned the drawing-
room, or bore the palm of academic strife. While
in the bloom and brilliancy of body and mind,
when most sensitive and alive to all the passionate
and beautiful associations of affection and of intellect, the spoiler stealthily crept in, but previously a light from heaven had entered his heart,
and therefore, while the malady built up the
barrier between time and his spirit, the patient
relied upon the hand that chastened him; he felt
that pain and weakness, and weariness and disappointment and death, are not fortuitous occur-
rences, but the process by which the wisdom of
God effects the weaning and separation of the
believing soul from sin, sorrow, and distracting
attachments, to fill it for ever with intelligence,
peace, and perfection. Hence, with becoming
composure, he submitted to the purifying trial of
his faith, and said, while his features reflected the

M

divine love which he contemplated—"Even so,
Father, for so it seemeth good in thy sight."   No
fever of the mind added to the hectic which consumed his body, and the disease was not only
better borne, but really much retarded and ame-
liorated by the " strong consolations" of Christian
faith.

CHAPTER VII.

IRRITABLE BRAIN, INSANITY, &c.

MANY terrible nervous diseases are but the natural disturbance of a bad conscience. Such a course of conduct before God and man as secure approval of heart, will often cure such diseases without the aid of the physician. The cordial of daily duty, properly fulfilled, is the proper remedy. How often have we seen the haggard hypochondriac, both in hut and mansion, cured of all his anomalous maladies by a true view of religion and by the activity which springs from it. The terrors that haunted his darkened spirit have been dissipated by the light of heaven; his shaken nerves have been tranquillized, and the peace of faith has brought new brightness into his eye; a pleasant buoyancy has lifted his heart, and a resistless impulse of good will has diffused a healthful vigour through every fibre and every feature. So powerful is the habit of a man's faith on his person, that sagacious physicians often correctly infer the religious state and persuasion from the patient's appearance.

M 2

That bodily disorder which favours the manifestation of the mind in an insane manner may be produced by any of our passions, when unrestrained by a holy understanding; the best blessings may thus be converted into curses—the best gifts into the most injurious agents. Some say religion is a frequent cause of insanity. No; true religion is the spirit of love, of power, and of a sound mind; ever active in diversified duties and delights, always busy in a becoming manner and in decent order. But the wild notions, unmeaning superstitions, spiritual bondage, unrequired and forbidden attempts to reconcile the rites and ceremonies which wayward men have substituted for the liberty of God, begin in disobedience and end in darkness. It is strange fire in the censer which brings down the flaming vengeance, and opens a passage to the infinite abyss.

Excessive employment of the body, and that anxiety which springs from too earnest a pursuit of our own wills, are, when acting together, exceedingly likely to disorder the organism of the mental faculties; and whether one be truly religious or only superstitious, the result will be the same; because excess of any kind is a direct infringement of the invariable law of God.

Delirium may arise either from mental stimulants or from mental sedatives, in a weakened and wearied state of the brain. In either case the same effects follow; as the organization is so disturbed that it consents not in due order to the force which, in its proper condition, is formed to actuate it, namely, the mind. To make a mental exertion when the brain is wearied or unduly excited, is only to aggravate disorder and endanger the fine fabric thus violently acted upon. Thus it is that men of mental determination, under the force and pressure of urgent business, instead of yielding to the indications of weariness, continue to work on till delirium takes the place of healthy attention. The secretary of an extensive and useful institution, for instance, suffers from bad health; his mind and heart find no rest at home; at this juncture the directors call for accounts and a multitude of correspondents are urgent for replies. He finds some one of these agents is guilty of defalcation. He grows miserable; his digestion fails, he appears flushed and flurried, his head aches, he can scarcely connect his thoughts, his hand trembles, he uses wrong words both in speaking and in writing; he retires, and immediately begins to connect the feeling of his own inability to attend to business with the idea of robbing his employers, and at length fancies that he is the defaulter, by whose case his mind has been excited. He thinks himself the guilty person, and, haunted by the worst consequent phantoms, he becomes intolerable to himself, and feels as if called on to expiate his crime by destroying his life with his own hand. His pious habit still prevails, and he executes the horrible deed in calm and devout resignation to what he deems the will of heaven. This is a true case, and is no uncommon result of disobedience to the natural law, which insists on our seeking rest when wearied, and submitting patiently to infirmity as our daily portion.

All disobedience to the Divine laws, whether natural or moral, must of course be inevitably followed by suffering and disorder; nor can any one who exposes himself to its causes be exempt, unless by miracle, from insanity or hallucination, as long as mind acts through matter, and manifests itself in keeping with its condition.

Remarkable intellectual energy is so often associated with enthusiasm or intensity of mental character and extravagance of conduct, that it has become a proverb:—"Great wit to madness is allied." And probably the excessive activity of mind sometimes springs from actual disorder of brain, although the habit and education of the will of the individual may enable him so far to control its influence as that a degree of disease which, in another worse trained, might produce decided symptoms of insanity, shall, in this case, only prove a powerful stimulus to manageable imagination. The susceptibility of genius to the ex-

citement of society generally betrays itself in
eccentricities, which minds less endowed regard
with amazement; as if these odd traits were some
inexplicable mystery and contradiction instead of
the necessary result of the nervous tension, to
which such morbid beings are constantly subject.
It may appear, at first sight, unreasonable to
connect genius with disease, but an intimacy with
the history of notable men will demonstrate their
relation to each other; not that they are necessarily associated, as cause and consequence, but
that the direct operation of intense motives, such
as stimulate master minds, leads to disorder of
the brain, and disorder of the brain reacts to
maintain a perverted bias or injurious habit of
application. Those who are restrained in their
ambitious or pleasurable pursuits by moral or
religious principles, are happily preserved from
the danger of catering to the public appetite for
marvellous, monstrous, and startling exhibitions
of talent; but gifted persons, who submit to the
enormous demand, and ransack the regions of
invention for new wonders and striking combinations, are always running the risk of losing the
mastery over their own faculties, simply because
it is a law of the human mental constitution to
confirm a chosen habit into an absolute necessity;
because the brain, constantly used in one manner, whether naturally or artificially, cannot act

in any other; but, enthralled by a task-tyrant of
its own choice, it works on in chains like a galley
slave, and dies early of its chosen toil. This effect
of habit in determining genius accounts for the
progress of deception under the control of design-
ing men of great enthusiasm, such as Mahomet
and Joseph Smith, the inventor of Mormonism.
They began by some trick to help themselves, and
thus discovering their power over the simple-
minded, they persisted in deception till they became unable to think or act but as deceivers. At
length, probably the habit was confirmed by their
becoming insane converts to their own lies, believing the whims of their own imaginations to be
the especial revelations of heaven. Like a horse
in a mill, the mind thus goes round and round in
the same circle, till it turns blind and incapable of
straight forward exertion. Its very dreams are of
the beaten track.

An accumulated irritability of brain results
from incessant effort of mind; and to such an
extent are poets subject to this infirmity that
they have won the cognomen of a distinct race—
genus irritabile. But all imprudent thinkers are
obnoxious to the same suffering. Even our great
philosopher, Newton, sometimes gave vent to ill-
temper or soothed his nerves by the bane of tobacco, instead of taking rest or appropriate change.
And many of our best artists, whether in words

or more solid materials, have been martyrs to head-ache and the fashion of excitement. Thus Wilkie was often obliged to shut himself up in a dark room, because light was too stimulant for his brain, and Paganini paid dearly for his consummate excellence as a musician. Speaking to a friend, he stated that he scarcely knew what sleep was; and his nerves were wrought to such almost preternatural acuteness, that harsh, even common sounds, often became torture to him. He was sometimes unable to bear a whisper in his room. His passion for music he described as an all-absorbing, a consuming one; in fact he looked as if no other life than that ethereal one of melody were circulating in his veins; but he added, with a glow of triumph kindling through deep sadness,—" *Mais c'est un don du ciel.*"*

Byron, after an intellectual debauch, was accustomed to mope in total laziness. What this intense poet says of himself is very instructive—"I feel a disrelish more powerful than indifference. If I rouse, it is into a fury. I presume I shall end like Swift—dying at top. But Swift had hardly begun life at the very period (thirty-three) when I feel quite an old sort of feel. I have been considering why I always awake at a certain hour in the morning and always in very bad spirits: I may say in actual despair and despondency in all

* Mrs. Hemans' Life.

respects.   I have drank fifteen bottles of soda water in one night after going to bed, and still been thirsty.   A dose of salts has the effect of a temporary inebriation like light champagne upon me.   But wine and spirits make me sullen and savage to ferocity; silent, however, and retiring, and not quarrelsome if not spoken to."

These facts prove that his genius was associated with a diseased brain, of which indeed he died; but whether the disease was the result of undue mental action, or the cause of it, we need not now inquire: it is sufficient to point out the connexion.   Byron is but a strong example of the poetic temperament, and in many respects of the other orders of genius also, for they are all distinguished by extraordinary determination of will; subject however to paroxysms, like an intermittent fever, a succession of cold and hot fits, with healthier intervals, since the nervous system will not tolerate a constant enthusiasm.   All violence is but the exception to natural order, and the mighty afflatus or mental inspiration, which the world so much admires, can no more be commanded or expected as a matter of course than can the hurricane or the earthquake, and their continuance is alike destructive.

Virgil's description of the inspired Pythoness, presents a glowing picture of the mind's excitement, kindling the body for a time into unnatural

action and then leaving it exhausted and powerless,
—an effect that equally follows every great, enthusi-
astic, intellectual or passionate exertion of the will.

> " Aloud she cries
> This is the time ! enquire your destinies.
> He comes ! behold the god !   Thus while she said,
> (And shivering at the sacred entry staid),
> Her colour changed ; her face was not the same,
> And hollow groans from her deep spirit came.
> Her hair stood up ; convulsive rage possessed
> Her trembling limbs ; and heaved her labouring heart,
> Greater than human kind she seemed to look,
> And with an accent more than mortal spoke ;
> Her staring eyes with sparkling fury roll,
> When all the god came rushing on her soul,
> Swiftly she turned and foaming as she spoke,
> At length her fury fell ; her foaming ceased
> And ebbing in her soul the god decreased."

The common sense of mankind, before the materialists extinguished the soul, which gave life even to
the doctrines of heathens, naturally ascribed all
bodily and mental agitations to some indwelling
spirit, and regarded visible actions as the result
of invisible agencies, so as always to connect the
physical with the spiritual; and doubtless, therefore, they more firmly realized the fact of their
immediate relation to an immaterial existence.   A
far more beautiful and ennobling philosophy was
theirs than the mere materialists enjoy, because
nearer that of divine truth than the notion that
traces mind no further than to chemical affinities,

and views the death of the vigilant soul in the destruction of its dwelling place.

Dr. Wollaston, who was a Christian philosopher, died of disease of the brain. He preserved to the close of his life the philosophic habit of observation which distinguished his character. Sublime is the lesson, to see how he exercised the higher faculties of his intellect in reasoning on the causes and progress of his malady in the disorder of his sensations, memory, and the power of motion, as it advanced in its incursion upon one part after another of those portions of the brain which subserve the mind in relation to will and consciousness. He noted the phenomena of death, as it gradually took possession of his body, and experimented on his faculties to ascertain the amount of living power remaining. Here we witness an intelligent being watching the gradual destruction of the instruments with which it was accustomed to seek and communicate intellectual enjoyment. The spirit takes its last look at its material residence, and seems voluntarily to withdraw from an abode so incommodious while reasoning about the causes of its unfitness. Up to the very verge of this life's horizon we see that the willing and reasoning man remains a willing and reasoning being still. Shall we dare to say we have traced the footsteps of that man to the limit of his being? As well might we say a star is extinguished be-

cause it has set to our sight. The invisible spirit
evinced itself here by using earthly elements, and
in wise communion with the wonders of creative
skill, and its departure was but an entrance into
existence more in keeping with its nature. What
the philosopher observed decaying was not himself,
the observer, and that which died, was not that
which enjoyed life.

CHAPTER VIII.

A GENERAL VIEW OF THE EFFECTS OF THE PASSIONS ON HEALTH.

OUR passions are the grand conservators as well as disturbers of the healthy action of our bodies; and they exercise so direct an influence over the functions of life as to be properly classified with medicinal agents. Indeed they often act with no less power than the most heroic medicines, and are as rapid, and sometimes as fatal in their operation, as prussic acid or any other deadly poison. A brief review of the prominent effects of our passions on our bodies will afford a striking illustration of the independent existence of the mind, and at the same time present a subject of the highest practical consideration. Medically speaking, the emotions are regarded either as depressing or exciting, — sedative or stimulant; but probably their influence, although always acknowledged, is yet too generally undervalued in the treatment of disease.

Hope is the cordial by which our benevolent Creator cheers every heart that is not resolutely set against the reception of his goodness. A remarkable, and consequently often-quoted instance, of the curative influence of hope occurred during the siege of Breda, in 1625, when the garrison was on the point of surrendering from the ravages of scurvy, principally induced by mental depression. A few phials of sham medicine were introduced, by order of the Prince of Orange, as an infallible specific. It was given in drops and produced astonishing effects. Such as had not moved their limbs for months before were seen walking in the streets—sound, straight, and well.

Not to refer to the long list of pseudo-miracles by royal touch and at the tombs of common saints, sight to the blind and hearing to the deaf, with the cure of every sickness, were said to have been conferred on the faithful devotees who flocked to the tomb of Abbè Paris, the famous Jansenist; and what is most extraordinary these cases were proved on the spot, before judges of integrity, attested by witnesses of credit in a learned age (A.D. 1724), and on the most eminent theatre in the world. Among a multitude of similar cures, it is testified that a hunch-backed girl was kicked and trampled into a beautiful shape, by being stretched on the ground, while a number of stout men trode and jumped with all their might on her stomach and ribs. The treatment was in all cases of so rough a kind that it required a confidence amounting to lunacy to submit to it, and the exercise of a power as supernatural at least, if not as deceptive, as Satan's, in order to survive it. However, as Pascal said, "we must believe those who are ready to have their throats cut to prove their faith." The priests appealed to the remains of their saint in attestation of their own sanctity, and of course miracles followed; and then what more natural than that the lame, the halt, and the blind, should, in hopeful crowds, surround the wonder-working bones of St. Paris? What more natural, except that many of them, under the violent persuasion of their own desire and many heavy blows, should speedily depart miraculously healed?

Eloquence is not needed to describe the mightiness of *Hope*. She speaks for herself to every mortal, and supplies, gratis, to every sufferer a well-authenticated universal remedy; far safer, indeed, without the vaunted vegetables, aloes, and gamboge than with them. It may be indulged with little risk, which cannot be said of whole-sale Morrisonian pill-taking, nor even of the recent but now exploded catholicon brandy and salt. Hope, like an angel, can concentrate her healing virtue in a homœopathic globule, or diffuse it through all the multitudinous baths, douches, and wet bandages of hydropathic establishments. Her bright face is seen in every stream. If we listen, we hear her voice when-ever the breath of heaven visits us. "Hope enchanted smiles and waves her golden hair," as she dances before us on the hills and in the vallies; health and laughter are in her steps, and while we gaze upon her joyous beauty a lithesome spirit animates our limbs, and the blooming hilarity of her features is reflected from our own.

Fear is also sometimes curative. The great Boerhaave had a number of patients seized with epileptic fits in an hospital, from sympathy with a person who fell down in convulsions before them. This physician was puzzled how to act, for the sympathetic fits were as violent and obsti-nate as those arising from bodily disease; but, reflecting that they were produced by impres-sion on the mind, he resolved to eradicate them by a still stronger impression, and so directed hot irons to be prepared and applied to the first person who subsequently had a fit; the consequence was that not a person was seized afterwards.

An officer in the Indian army was confined to his bed by asthma and could only breathe in an erect posture; but a party of Mahrattas broke into the camp, and fearing certain death, he sprang out with amazing activity, mounted his horse and used his sword with great execution, although the day before he could not draw it from its scabbard. A beautiful example of the curative operation of affectionate apprehension is given by Wordsworth, in his singular story of the Idiot Boy.

Hildanus relates that a man, disguised as a ghost, took another labouring under severe gout from his bed and carried him on his back down the stairs, dragging his painful and swollen feet down the steps and placed him on the ground. He immediately recovered the use of his limbs, and swiftly ran up stairs under the strongest terror, and never had the gout again. In these cases fear acted with all the stimulating force of necessity, which is proverbially powerful.

But the gentler and more pleasing emotions sometimes effect the same apparently miraculous restoration. The case of an old man, who laboured under shaking palsy, was related by Mr. Kingdon, at the Medical Society of London. This person had been long unable to walk. The child of a friend was admitted to see him, and so greatly delighted was he that he arose, walked across the room, took some paper, went to another part of the room, filled the paper with small shells, gave it to the child, and then sat down as paralytic as before.

Terror causes the blood suddenly to leave the extreme parts of the frame; the countenance becomes livid, the brain excited, the large arteries distended, the heart swells, the eyes start, the muscles become rigid or convulsed, and faintness, and perhaps sudden death, ensue. Fear, whether it be from a real or an imaginary object, is equally influential on the body. A woman had her gown bitten by a dog; she had heard of hydrophobia, and immediately fancied that she had it; and, what is most surprising, she actually died of symptoms so like canine madness that skilful physicians could not discover any difference. John Hunter, the celebrated anatomist, attributed the disease of the heart of which he ultimately died in a fit of anger, to the fear of having caught hydrophobia while dissecting the body of a patient who died of that disease. Dr. Holland states that a young man was so severely affected by the continual intrusion of illusory images of a frightful kind, that in a few weeks his hair turned from black to white.

As recollected ideas often follow the same train as when first impressed, a lively remembrance of past effects is apt to renew the same actions of the body. Probably the same state of nerve is again produced. Hence the dispositions to repeat actions in an accustomed manner. Van Swietan informs us of a child, being frightened into epilepsy by a large dog leaping on it, in whom the fit returned whenever the dog was heard to bark. Had the child been capable of mental effort, the association might perhaps have been broken; as we find that epilepsy is often arrested by diverting the nervous power by some strong voluntary action of the body, or other determination of the will; and hence too, several popular remedies for this disease exert a powerful influence over it, by their effect on the imagination; as that of the hand of a felon, recently hanged, applied to the patient's brow while on the scaffold. The hand of a murderer applied while hanging from the gibbet is said to be especially efficacious. For the same purpose Pliny advised the blood of a dying gladiator drunk warm, and Scribonius Largus directs a portion of his liver to be eaten. Aretæus prefers the raw heart of a coot and the brain of a vulture. The nail taken from the arm of a crucified malefactor was an efficacious amulet according to Alexander. Not two centuries since the authentic remedy among English physicians was the lichen which grew on a decaying human skull.

Other nervous disorders are cured on the principle of breaking the mental association; thus cramp is cured by rings made from the nails of an old coffin, and all sorts of nerve-ache are now within reach of art, since the magic galvanic rings of copper and zinc, a mixture which must have prevailed in the constitutions of their inventors, are declared to be nothing short of miraculous, but of course they are intended especially for those who have only heard of science.

There is no doubt however that a feeling of awe will modify the circulation, and probably the mystery-men or medicins of the American Indians, with its help, perform cures almost as wonderful as those ascribed to Parr's life pills or any other imposing pretension. Hence also the potency of charms. This feeling of awe seems to partake somewhat of the nature of horror, which is demonstrated to act powerfully on the blood vessels, as is seen not only in the pallid appearance of individuals suffering from it, but also in the common success of a vulgar remedy for hæmorrhage, namely a living toad hung about the neck. The disgusting contact almost instantly arrests slight bleedings. But perhaps this remedy is not more efficacious than the cold key; and it certainly is not more in demand, and therefore it may be presumed not more successful among our peasantry than the village blood-stauncher, who is generally some shrewd old woman that sees a little through her neighbours, and is near akin to a witch. She is "great mystery," as the Indians say, and arrests bleedings by an awful manner, a muttered unmeaning prayer, and a call for faith.

Extreme joy and extreme terror act in a manner equally energetic. Occasionally the exhaustion produced by them is so sudden that the nervous system seems to be discharged of its power in an instant. Culprits have received the tidings of pardon, when standing under the gallows, and have fallen dead in a moment as by a lightning stroke.

That most stimulating of the passions, *anger*, rouses the heart, produces a glow all over the body, especially in the face; causes the eyes to glare; strengthens the voice, and increases the muscular power; hence it has now and then suddenly cured gout and palsy, but much more frequently it has proved fatal, by rupturing some blood vessel. The blood, fevered by rage, rushes with delirium over the burdened brain; the heart for a while beats fiercely but "the acrid bile soon chokes the fine ducts;" every vessel is exhausted; the irritability ceases; every muscle shakes; the whole strength is prostrated; and then, if palsy do not happen, obstinate faintings ensue; then convulsions—then death—and the angry man meets his God face to face.

Broussais and other eminent physiologists are of opinion that rage is capable of generating a most virulent and subtle poison, especially in the saliva. They refer to numerous instances in which wounds from enraged animals have been followed by effects only to be accounted for by supposing a virus communicated. This opinion coincides with vulgar belief, and if true, as facts seem to affirm, the power of the mind in altering the chemistry of life in a direct manner is thus most clearly demonstrated. But indeed the same fact is equally evinced by the common influence of emotion over secretion. The classical reader will remember Ovid's fine description of Envy.

Pallor in ore sedet ; macies in corpore toto ;
Nusquam recta acies ; livent rubigine dentes :
Pectora felle virent ; lingua est suffusa venemo.

The description of a well-known disease will not be here out of place. It begins with indulgence in despondency, then follow loss of appetite, constant pain in the stomach, difficulty of breathing, paleness of the face and palms of the hands, whiteness of the tongue with inky spots on it, white lips, and inability to move. Then the white of the eye becomes glassy, the skin turns of an olive colour and cold to the touch, water collects in every part of the body and the sufferer cannot breathe except in an erect position. The glands then become inflamed, the liver hardened; and the blood, poor, vapid and colourless, no longer stimulates the heart, and death soon terminates the scene. This is not the home sickness, or *nostalgia*, which sprung up among the Swiss soldiers at the sound of their native music, from a passion for home; and which the kindliest associations often failed to cure, without returning to the hills and vallies, the sights and sounds, the domestic en-

joyments and familiar delights, so endeared to
the heart by the strong sympathies of childhood,
as to localize the spirit of the man and fill his
memory with so delicious a sense of what he loved
and had lost, that his soul could perceive no joy
but in home, sweet home! The malady above
described is a more violent disease of the same
kind, and it is dignified by the title *Cachexia
Africana,* because, alas! it has killed thousands
on thousands of the children of Africa when
" forced from home and all its pleasures."

Are there not however many among us no less
pitiable, the victims of frivolity, of fashion, of evil
genius, of anxious and ungodly trade, and of
every vice; led captive at the will of him who
pays his slaves for all their toils with grievous
penalty and death, without the hope of home
beyond it.

The slow fever of *anxiety* presents the Protean
symptoms which everywhere obtrude themselves.

" The broad consumptive plague
Breathes from the city to the farthest hut."

And its ravages are miserably visible in the union
houses, dispensaries, and hospitals of our land.
Every madhouse also furnishes instances of its
effects; and, moreover, strangely presents the
most terrible examples of remorse and religious
despair; proving that Christianity is often taught
by mistaken men rather as a system of terror than

as good news of gracious forgiveness to all those who faithfully repent.

Fear and anxiety affect all the functions of the body but especially of the stomach. They seem to suppress the secretion of the fluid on which digestion depends and also arrest the flow of saliva. A curious illustration of this fact is afforded in the method which the conjurers in India sometimes adopt for detecting theft among servants. When a robbery has been committed a conjurer is sent for, and great preparations are made. If in a few days the property be not restored, he proceeds with his mysterious operations, one of which is as follows :—The suspected are all required to masticate a quantity of boiled rice for some time, and then to spit it upon separate leaves for inspection. He examines the masticated rice very knowingly, and immediately points out the culprit; the rice which he masticated being perfectly dry, while that which was masticated by the others is moistened by saliva.

Deferred and fruitless longing for a beloved object is a frequent malady which always tends to produce a remarkable deterioration of the blood, thus of course impairing the function of every organ. As the nervous system is most susceptible, the evil is first revealed by distressing nervous sensations. All periods and all conditions of life are liable to this disease; but the more artificial the society the more prevalent the malady; that being considered the most natural society in which the natural affections are most suitably engaged. The prosperous fulfilment of our proper desires is not only the best preservation of the joys of relationship and the blessings of the social compact, but the best security for the health of body and of mind, both in parent and offspring; for the state of the blood, on which health mainly depends, is influenced almost as much by our feelings as by our food.

The grand struggle of the multitude is excited neither by ambition nor covetousness; nor that nicer torment, a morbid love of approbation, which racks the sensitive genius; nor by the delirium of an entrancing affection, nor by the tyranny of grosser passion;—but the common aim of the majority in their daily toil, is rather for means to sustain a bare and comfortless existence. The weariness of the scarcely successful effort is visible in almost every face. The vast increase of heart and nervous diseases arises from the distracting excitement and stretch of mind which now prevails throughout society, especially in large cities, where great competition exists, and where an uncertain commerce furnishes a precarious support, and wealth and pride too often take mean advantages of laborious poverty.

The votaries of pleasure are scarcely more exposed to the causes of mental disquietude than the devotees of Mammon, and both alike waste the energies of life in excitement, and alike suffer the penalty of breaking those laws which naturally regulate the uses both of mind and body. The gambling spirit as constantly haunts the exchange and corn market as the play-table; and, by perplexing and distracting the mind, soon saps the basis of health and anticipates old age. Hence, in large commercial towns, we often witness even in persons who have barely reached the middle period of life, the haggard face, sunken eye, hoary hair, and feeble gait, which properly belong to "wearied eld." Nor can the results be surprising to those who reflect that anxiety is but a chronic kind of fear; a sort of intermittent fever or ague, which as manifestly disorders the circulation and secretions as that which arises from the poisonous malaria of the marshes, and which is scarcely more deadly than that of the market, in these days of desperate speculation and grasping monopoly.

As Syrach says, " Sorrow also killeth many people, and melancholy consumeth marrow and bone." We have all heard of those who have become

"Grey haired with anguish in a single night."

But that is but a small part of the bodily evidence of mental agony.

Grief has a very marked influence over the cir-

N 2

culation; probably by its direct action on the heart, which may be so violently affected as really to break, not metaphorically but physically. Prolonged distress of mind invariably produces a great preponderance of the venous over the arterial blood; hence there arises a general feebleness. We are assured, on the testimony of their medical attendants, that convicts frequently die of broken hearts, and it requires more than ordinary care and skill to restore them to any degree of health, if once attacked by illness; as the absence of hope, especially among those transported for life, causes them to sink rapidly, whatever be the disease. They seldom recover, or, if partially restored, it is only to relapse from the slightest circumstances, and such as would not in the least affect persons enjoying liberty and hope.

Strong emotion often produces the germ of disease, which for a long time may not become apparent. The majority of what are called nervous diseases are probably of this class. Some grief, like a thorn at the heart, as Hippocrates says, by its secret and incessant irritation, gradually wears out the vital energy. Some vulture preys upon almost every heart, and it needs not the pride and ambition of a Napoleon, fastened to the lonely rock, to feel its gnawings, for disappointment as keenly follows every intense and absorbing passion.

Every part of the body testifies to the potency of emotions over the organism of life, though the physiologist may not always detect their effects in visible lesions or alterations. The first causes, or earliest physical impressions of disorder, are indeed beyond the ken of the dissector. In vain he searches into minute anatomy for the cause of functional derangement; it must be sought among agents which he cannot handle. An idea has frequently force enough to prostrate the strongest man in a moment. A word has blasted all his dearest, fondest, most habitual hopes. His only child has died—the partner of his life is snatched away;—he has but heard it; nothing has touched his body, but the "iron has entered his soul." He reels—he trembles—some demon grasps his brain—sleep is gone—he dares not look at the light.—A dull pain and a heavy cloud fix themselves over his eyes, and if the efforts of nature and art are unavailing, or if the balmy spirit of religion breathe not healing through his soul and speedily bind up the broken heart, some fatal malady of the brain more or less rapidly ensues, and the man of energy and affection becomes an outcast from society till death releases his spirit.

Next to the brain the stomach suffers from continued mental distress. The appetite fails; digestion is suspended; atrophy succeeds, and perhaps some nerve - ache racks the sufferer. Sometimes pulmonary consumption, or disease of the heart, the liver, or the bowels is induced. The secretions are of course proportionally affected. Thus the milk of a nurse is often entirely suppressed by mental disquietude. Hence a nervous excitable woman is hardly fit to suckle her own children; for the fluid that should nourish her infant undergoes so many changes, from the mother's mental variations, as greatly to distress the child and perhaps even to destroy it. Ninety-eight out of a hundred deaths from convulsions are of children, thus proving them to be especially liable to this disorder; and as the majority die in early infancy, it is not unlikely that the state of · the mother's mind may be the secret cause of this unnatural mortality.

Under mental depression the nervous energy becomes exhausted, the conservative power of nature is wanting, and the body is rendered especially obnoxious to external influences.

Captain Ross, in the narrative of his arctic voyage, particularly alludes to the circumstance of mental depression increasing susceptibility to cold. The disastrous retreat from Moscow also affords a striking and extensive instance. This kind of susceptibility to "the skyey influences" is most marked, but it equally exists in other forms; thus those who are depressed by any cause are most likely to take contagious diseases.

Now look at him who is emphatically the miser: that is the wretch. He seems as if all his affections had been congealed by a dip in Lethe, as Dr. M. Good observes. Yet some demon of anxiety, some cunning fiend, sits like a nightmare on his bosom and will not let him sleep, while whispering in his ear of robberies and of destitution. No cordial cheers—no wealth makes him comfortable—he grows thinner and thinner —his limbs totter and his nerves ache. Even if the charitable, whom he cheats, consent to feed him, though in the home of plenty, he cannot gather strength; his soul starves him. This poor pitiable being has been the subject of sarcasm from age to age; but many who laugh and point the finger at him are doubtless his descendants, for they bear a strong family likeness in their features, even to him of whom Valerius Maximus relates, that he took advantage of a famine to sell a mouse for two hundred pence, and then died famished with the money in his pocket.

Duty to our neighbour, our country, and our God, requires us to be diligent in business and fervent in spirit. With a right motive we shall find our utmost efforts to be healthy and happy; but are there not many, however, who ask not with a mockery of prayer for their daily bread, until they have plotted some scheme upon their beds by which they may file a fortune from the wages of industry, or cheat their less crafty brethren of some part of their due portion? How can these be healthy? Perhaps it is possible that such contrivers may be rubicund in their success, but it is more likely that the money-mania will at last absorb all the cheering springs of kindly sympathy, and leave them weak and weary in the dry desert of their selfishness,— their whole being a disease.

This is a common termination of a vicious course, whatever form of selfishness the vice assume; for vice is always selfish, and therefore apt to be increasingly anxious and wretched, till habit dries the heart up in despair.

CHAPTER IX.

SYMPATHY.

SYMPATHY is the natural check which the Almighty puts upon uncharitable self. In spite of themselves there are few who have not felt compassion for others. This affords a beautiful proof both of the beneficence of our Maker and of the power of mind over the body.

Pity, like love, imparts a sedate tenderness to the carriage, and if it cannot be relieved the face becomes pale and wan, the appetite fails, and the slumber is invaded with frightful dreams, and thus a broken heart from pity as from grief is no fiction.

Mr. Quain detailed the following case of sympathy at the Westminster Medical Society. A gentleman who had constantly witnessed the sufferings of a friend afflicted with stricture of the æsophagus, had so great an impression made on his nervous system, that after some time he experienced a similar difficulty of swallowing, and ultimately died of the spasmodic impediment produced by merely thinking of another's pain.

A curious and interesting effect of pathetic feeling is the production of tears, which are never generated but by sorrow or sympathy. There is a particular nerve supplying that part which causes the formation of tears, and it seems to be naturally stimulated only by the suffering of the mind. It is commonly observed that deep grief is apt to be dangerous if the brain be not relieved by tears; in fact, it indicates that the blow has been so severe as to paralize that part of the nervous system which causes them to flow. Hence we so often hear lamentations from the wounded heart that it can obtain no relief from its overwhelming sorrow, because the fountain of tears seems dried up.

There is a form of sympathy which compels us to imitate what we witness in others. This tendency is greatly aggravated under certain circumstances, as when persons are secluded from the domestic and social duties of life. Thus a French medical practitioner of great merit relates, that, in a convent of nuns, one of the fair inmates was seized with a strange impulse to mew like a cat, and soon the whole sisterhood followed her example, and mewed regularly every day for hours together. This diurnal caterwauling astounded the neighbourhood, and did not cease to scandalize more rational Christians, until the nuns were informed that a company of soldiers were to sur-

round the convent and to whip all the holy sisterhood with rods till they promised to mew no more.
A remedy which would be equally serviceable in
many other mental epidemics.

Cardan relates that, in another nunnery, a
sister was impelled to bite her companions, and
this disposition also spread among the sisterhood;
but instead of being confined to one nunnery, it
spread from cloister to cloister throughout the
whole of Europe. There is a kind of biting
mania, not confined to nunneries or to the fair
sex, and which may often be witnessed in almost
every coterie; it is backbiting; a malignant sort
of insanity, which spreads worse than the plague,
and disorders alike the body and the mind, both
collectively and individually.

Morbid and imitative sympathy is scarcely less
powerful among men than women, but it usually
takes a different form in the different sexes: a
good example has already been given in the case
of epileptic fits.

The dancing mania of the fourteenth century
infected men almost as readily as women. We
have but to witness a congregation of Jumpers at
their devotions, or even a mob of senseless parti-
zans at a stoutly contested election, to be convinced that the contagion of sympathy finds the
presence of the lordly sex no barrier to its exten-
sion. The evils of this kind of contagion, in con-

nexion with irrational enthusiasm, whether excited by true religion or by delusive assumptions, are of a nature to demand our most serious consideration, because the interests of truth are often sacrificed in consequence of confounding her accidental with her constant effects. In 1800, a blaze of apparently religious enthusiasm spread with great velocity through many parts of the United States. It began in a crowded congregation, who were rendered peculiarly susceptible by extreme fatigue and ignorance. After remaining in the same spot day and night, instead of worshipping, they commenced crying, laughing, singing, and shouting with every variety of convulsive contortion and gesticulation. They continued to act from necessity whatever character they had assumed from choice, and the disease extended in every direction with vast rapidity; as an affected person frequently communicated it to the greater part of a crowd collected by curiosity around him.

Children are more especially liable to this sort of symyathy, of which instances must be familiar to every reader. The fact, however, is of vast importance in connexion with the training of children, as a single evil example may counteract all our teaching. The imitative propensity is frequently exhibited in the diseases of children. A writer in the British and Foreign Medical Review states that he was consulted respecting a child who, when spoken to, instead of answering always repeated what was said. Degrees of this disease are very common. The same writer mentions a case, elsewhere published, in which an adult had from infancy irresistibly imitated all the muscular movements of those about him. When this dotterel-like propensity was forcibly restrained he complained that his heart and brain were vexed.

It is this imitative tendency which favors the rapid propagation of fanatic outrage, whether political or religious, whether of Jumpers or of Jansenists. But happily the susceptibility of those who so readily submit to outward impressions, and yield their souls to the government of transitory impulses instead of abiding principles, furnishes in itself a check to their extravagance, since some new form of such folly is ever presenting itself, and their nervous systems are ever open to fresh sympathies; so that succeeding excitements destroy each other, and error, always imitating and never self-possessed, assumes as many shapes as the father of lies himself,—" every thing by turns but nothing long." Truth alone is qualified to settle, compose, and establish the form of society, and to hold as well as to obtain universal dominion over the minds and bodies of mankind. We are naturally organized in sympathy rather with the holy than the evil; as we see that children, not infected by bad example, always love the good and beautiful. We may therefore believe that when society shall be more imbued with the practical spirit of truth, each succeeding generation shall sympathetically, as well as from conviction, exhibit more perfectly the beauties of individual and social obedience to divine law, which is the proper basis of education, and requires all the superstructure to be conformed to its outline. Instruction in all knowledge and action will be successful only in proportion as rule and example are divested of the disguises with which men have concealed Truth, the most persuasive and engaging of all teachers, because really the sole mistress of our constitutional sympathies.

We are governed by appearances, and we seem intuitively to act upon this principle; and, without intending it, we express the pleasure we feel and desire to convey by meeting our friend with a constant smile. The outward signs of passion and emotion, which are so wonderfully expressed in every attitude and feature, constitute the language of the soul, the bond of interest and union between mind and mind. Men are qualified to influence others just in proportion as they are gifted with the power of feeling lofty emotions and of expressing them with anatomical precision, and appropriate compass of face, of voice, and of action. Hence the success of the actor's, or the orator's art depends on the facility with which his nerves and muscles assume a truthfulness of expression in the embodiment of feeling, which indeed can never be fully and satisfactorily accomplished without an actual participation in some degree of the passion represented; for the effort to imitate will every now and then be manifest where the feeling does not somewhat animate the gesture and expression. The best actors, therefore, are those that are least like actors, and it is a fact that such as have been most successful on the stage have often been nearly unconscious of acting, in their realizing conception of the scene in which they placed themselves and the characters they have assumed. Thus real tears are not uncommon with a good tragedian, nor is hearty laughter with a comic actor. Preachers might here learn a useful lesson. It is in vain for a man to endeavour to persuade others till he has persuaded himself. He cannot convince his audience that he is influenced by emotion unless they see it; which they cannot while he is merely endeavouring to imitate the action that belongs to emotion, instead of feeling what he speaks. Real hypocrites, are really poor orators, and they are always ready to suspect more successful persuaders of more art than themselves, whereas they have only more nature active within them. The

unfeeling preacher egregiously fails, and so does
he, however feeling, who imitates others instead
of expressing himself. If, however, he suitably
contemplate the subject or passion that he would
describe, and make an effort to regard it sted-
fastly, he will at length be moved by it as he
would by a living example of the passion or subject before his face; for he cannot fix his attention
sufficiently on a subject not interesting to him.
His own sympathies will thus be roused, and he
will also rouse others almost to the extent of his
own enthusiasm, if his power of language correspond with his feeling, which it generally will. This
want of actual emotion in the speaker causes the
sublimest truths and the most thrilling relations
of great facts to fall lifelessly from the lips, so
that the sentences uttered come forth like wreaths
of sleepy mist instead of living forms of light.

Those who are most commanding among orators
do not appear to be so much addressing their
audience as to be contemplating and expressing
some subject of vast interest to themselves, and
which inspires their very souls and features with
language and significance, like a Pythoness. It
is this kind of inspiration with which an audience
is most enthralled, as those can testify who have
heard such men as Robert Hall. But the force
and fervour of the possessing influence must be

visible in the countenance, as well as heard in the intonations of the voice. The kindling eye, especially, must speak.

The features, when excited, are so nicely expressive of the variations in mental emotion, that by looking on them we at once read the state of the mind in which the individual appears before us, unless indeed he artfully conceal himself, but even then constraint will be visible.

The skill of the painter is most highly evinced by his seizing the evanescent play of feeling, which, though unstable as a ray of light upon the trembling water, yet in a moment reveals the emotion of the soul; and it is the exquisite accordancy between this index and the intelligence that moves it, which characterizes the man of eloquent features, and imparts, with the addition of appropriate language and utterance, an almost supernatural fascination to the gifted orator. Even without the auxiliaries of living energy, tone, and language, the actions of the muscles of the face and eyes are so marvellously fashioned to respond to the touch of passion on their nerves, and so completely calculated to excite our sympathy, that the features even of a dead man may be automatically played upon by galvanism, so that spectators shall feel their sensibilities uncontrollably disturbed. Dr. Ure relates an instance in which rage, horror, despair, anguish, and

ghastly smiles united their hideous expression in
the face of a murderer lately executed, in a manner surpassing the wildest representations of a
Fuseli or a Kean. So powerful was the effect
that several of the spectators were forced to leave
the room from terror, and one gentleman fainted.

The missionary martyr, Williams, gives a good
example of the power of acting in exciting sympathy. During the launching of a ship by the
natives of Eimeo, an old warrior stood on a little
eminence to animate the men at the ropes. "His
action was most inspiring. There seemed not a
fibre of his frame which he did not exert; and
merely from looking at him, I felt as though I
was in the very act of pulling."

Young children are strongly affected by facial
expression, and they learn the features of passion long before they learn any other part of its
language. Their imitative faculties are so active
and their sympathies so acute, that they uncon-
sciously assume the expression of face which they
are accustomed to see and feel. Hence the importance that children be habituated to kindli-
ness, beauty and intellect in those with whom
they are domesticated. Even their playthings
and pictures should be free from depraved meaning and violent expression, if we wish them to
be lovely; and all the hideous, grotesque, and
ludicrous portraiture, which now vulgarize the

public mind, should be excluded from the nursery. The gothic and superstitious condition of mind will return with the prevalence of pictorial deformities, and the demand for the unnatural will increase with the continuance of degraded art; for which deforming epidemic there can be no remedy, but in familiarizing the common mind with nobler objects.

CHAPTER X.

SOLITUDE.

It is by sympathy with each other that minds become either corrupted or improved; and however advantageous occasional solitude may be for the purpose of familiarizing the mind with its own actings, and however necessary it may be for the arrest of pernicious associations, still it is not by solitude, but by mind acting on mind, through the living medium of sight, sound, and touch, that erroneous humanity is led to right thinking. Where shall it find a pathway out of the mysterious desert of its temptations, while left alone or without a companion, except the tempter? It was in the separation of those whom God had joined together that the serpent beguiler was first able to triumph; and when a human being is alone that evil spirit still haunts him with the likeliest hope of conforming the soul to his own purposes.

Without suitable response to his social desires, the mind of fallen man will conjure up a thousand beings to converse with its thoughts, and to give sentiment and language even to inanimate objects. All the world is alive to man's imagina-

tion. Hence the solitudes of the wilderness, where
the Indian wanders alone, are peopled by him
with spirits; and hence, too, haunted places
abound in the traditions of thinly populated dis-
tricts, and among those people whose business
requires them to pass much time in solitary walks
and watchings among hills and vallies, where no
sign of human association breaks the monotony of
speechless existence. The Indian saying is true,
" Fast in the wilderness and dream of spirits."
This superstitious tendency is equally manifested,
whatever the nature of the solitude, that is, if the
mind be developed, and has not previously been
imbued with truth and holiness. The madden-
ing terrors of young criminals who are confined
to solitary cells, is thus to be explained.

Probably the solitude of stone walls is the most
terrible of desolations; for living nature, however
wild, will suggest some thought of a benevolent
and protecting spirit. But when vice is doomed
to the dungeon, to hear no voice save that of a
guilty conscience, and to see no smile but the
ghastly smile of despair, what kind of superstition
can there enter but that which makes visible the
darkness of hell and prompts the madman to seek
refuge from his tormentors in self-murder. An
author, of no common power and sagacity, tells
us that, when at New York, he visited the prison
where they carry out the solitary system, and

held the following brief and significant conversation with the turnkey.

"Pray why do they call this place the tombs?"

"Well, it's the cant name.

"I know it is. Why?"

"Some suicides happened here when it was first built. I expect it come about from that."

I saw just now that the man's clothes were scattered about the floor of his cell. "Dont you oblige prisoners to be orderly and put such things away?" "Where should they put 'em?" "Not on the ground, surely: what do you say to hanging them up?"

He stops and looks round to emphasize the answer: "Why I say that's just it. When they had hooks they would hang themselves, so they are taken out of every cell and there's only the marks left where they used to be!"

The isolation of a human spirit is worse than death, for the author of humanity has constituted it for intercourse, and every where in nature has provided it with scope and occasion to receive and communicate impulses of affection and of thought. Even in hell there is companionship. Evil spirits are attracted to each other, and are permitted to know so much of mercy as to wander even in legions together. They associate in their misery and their mischief, but man has invented a new mode of punishment and destruction, by imprison-

ing his wayward and ignorant brother in a tomb :
"a breathing man gifted with voice and hearing
is built up in a silent solitary sepulchre of stone,"
as if to bury his very soul; since there the pulse
of another heart may not beat, and there the
lonely spirit, thus cut off from the enjoyment of
its own faculties, is tormented to madness by the
clash of thoughts and passions without aim or
object. The improvement of even a wise man
without any other fellowship than his own reflection is impossible. He may arrange his knowledge and devise new schemes, but his heart is
never the better, unless busied for the benefit of
others, or, talking as it were with angels, he
learns of them, or at least is roused by fellowship
with feelings that neither originate nor terminate
in self. If then the man accustomed to secluded
meditation gains no moral progress or advancement but in the interchange of mind with mind,
are we to expect the miserable being, who perhaps
by his very criminalty has demonstrated that he
is so uncontrollably excited by association, so
mastered by his passions that his own safety is of
small moment in comparison with the pleasure of
pleasing his associates,—are we to expect such a
being to be conducted into right thinking, feeling, and acting, without another mind to approve,
direct, and encourage him in his aspirations after
a higher place in the scale of moral existence?

What is needed in such a case is surely a friend,
—one with a heart and soul, capable of appreci-
ating the value of a redeemed and immortal spirit,
of proving a true Christian devotedness to the
service of a sinful man, and of loving him in
hope of what he may be hereafter. Thus will he
be drawn, if at all, by the mighty gentleness of
heaven's charity, to follow in sympathy, love, and
veneration, from the depths of vicious debasement
even to the gates of heaven, and into its very
glory. It is kindness that wins the heart. Hence
the apostolic exhortation—"Be followers of God,
as dear children." Captain Sir W. E. Parry,
commenting on these words, observes, "there is
perhaps nothing even in the whole compass of
Scripture more calculated to awaken contrition in
the hardest heart than the Parable of the Prodigal
Son. I knew a convict in New South Wales in
whom there appeared no symptom of repentance,
in other respects, but who could never hear a sermon or comment on this parable without bursting
into an agony of tears, which I witnessed on
several occasions. Truly he who spoke 'it knew
what was in man."

Rational retirement is impossible to the irreli-
gious mind. Such a mind perceives not the
proper relation of any thing, and dares not dwell
alone for the purpose of contemplation; for all it
can feel in solitude is the necessity of keeping up

courage by some effort, like a school-boy at night among the tombs. The spontaneous phantasmagoria of the vigilant and guilty spirit rise like unaccountable goblins, unless such a one is busy with his senses. Solitude is therefore terror and madness to the uninformed; but let a man be suitably instructed and furnished with the proper means of happy mental occupation, and then occasional seclusion will soothe and elevate his spirit. Retirement from the world is indeed the way to heaven, and it is when the soul is alone in the agony of its heavy necessities that God and the Son of God visit it with salvation. The separation of man from all his sympathies is death; and solitude is fit for man only when man is fit for fellowship with God. But yet the Almighty has instituted separation in the dying hour, only to conduct the retiring and confiding spirit to the socialties of a sublimer life.

The deadening influence of silent confinement is of course most rapidly destructive to the powers of both mind and body in youth, at which period nature is active with no other purpose but pleasure and development. These being suddenly arrested, the mental faculties, as well as the limbs, become useless. If not speedily emancipated, the child thus unnaturally treated will soon be found both an idiot and a cripple. Such a process is like reducing an expanded human being to the state of Caspar Hauser, who being concealed from his infancy in a small cellar, there grew to the stature of a young man, with less of bodily activity and less of appearance of mind than a child at its mother's breast. "The life of his soul could be compared only to the life of an oyster, which, adhering to its rock, is sensible of nothing but the absorption of its food, and perceives only the eternal uniform dashing of the waves, and in its narrow shell finds no room even for the most confined idea of a world without it, still less of any thing above the earth and above all worlds." Yet this interesting youth, under the benevolent but very defective teaching of kindly associations, afterwards manifested such exquisite delicacy of intellect, conjoined with such pure and beautiful blendings of affection, that those who could best read the character of his soul most tenderly loved him.

Children become idiots in continued solitary confinement, but adults more frequently become either suicides or madmen; because in the former there is the absence of guilty habit, but the will in the latter had been long perverted and bent upon the attainment of some specific object, in which they promised themselves especial pleasure. Even self-amendment and escape from the misery of their guilty course had often been hoped for as an end with many of the worst inmates of our prisons; when, therefore, such wretched men are deprived of the most distant expectation of being in any way respected or beloved, it is no wonder they become insane.

Man, in constant banishment from fellowship, is almost beyond the reach of hope, and in proportion as he is without hope, he is without the natural stimulus and inducement to self-correction. A human being so situated is already in the position of a melancholy madman. The one is deprived of all hope of enjoyment by disease, the other by his fellow-man; and in both cases, if the cause continue, the end can only be entire loss of intellect or else suicide; for the brain and nerves are robbed of their proper stimuli and the body becomes the pregnant source of agonizing sensations.

It is by activity that our faculties are preserved as well as developed, and their proper action is always agreeable. Life, in fact, is not properly maintained unless in some measure pleasurable. A feeling of unfitness for life always seizes the heart that is robbed of hope, and whenever despair gets possession, the soul desires death and struggles for oblivion. There can be no spontaneous remedy in our disordered nature for the terrors of guilt, but if we possess a true faith despair appears impossible. Belief in God, as He is, not according to this mode or that, but simply as our God for ever, is the only cure for every thorough heart trouble.   o 2

CHAPTER XI.

THE GOVERNMENT OF THE PASSIONS.

WE cannot doubt that, as the life of this flesh hangs on a breath, so the power of controlling thought hangs on some delicate arrangement of atoms, with which the soul is so connected as to move it and to be moved by it. The difference between the sublimest philosopher and the most grovelling idiot, in regard to the exhibition and enjoyment of intellect, is, as far as we can discover, but the difference in their respective organization, and its state of health. This humbling view ought to cure us of intellectual conceit; for who dares despise his brother's understanding; when he reflects that the Divine mind will hereafter judge us not for lack of power but for its abuse; not according to what we have not, but according to what we have; and will distribute new endowments as each may have employed the capacity he held. The decisive crisis is but a result. How silly then is that common adulation of talent which regards not moral principle, and values the play of wit more than a Godlike will, although this is indeed the only true dignity of our nature. What mere cant of bigotry and carping criticism must that be which would alike depress all minds to their own low, dull, flat, unprofitable level of formality, as if the diversified workmanship of the Infinite could all be trimmed into the same shape by conceited man. As well may we endeavour to reduce creation to a monotony as to bring all minds to perceive and act in the same manner. The spirit of each must vary as much from all others in power and intelligence, as the material medium, through which it works, must differ from all others in construction and circumstances.

The body is only a convenient form which the spirit uses, and we have the highest authority for believing that many spirits may occupy and employ the same body. Nor can we discover any thing in nature that renders it difficult to credit this fact. Some persons with most unphilosophical audacity have however denied its possibility, but at least it behoves them first to prove that they understand the mode of spiritual existence and operation before they contradict the literal force of the New Testament, from which we learn that, if we use not our bodies according to divine law they will be employed by other spirits to dishonour and destruction. But in no circumstances in which the moral integrity of the soul can be tried, does it necessarily succumb to the seduc-

tions of the body, nor, with right knowledge and
reliance, to the persuasions of perverse spirits.

"Who reigns within himself and rules
Passions, desires and fears, is more than king."—*Milton.*

But how are our passions to be governed except by a dominant principle or attachment to
some mighty truth, by which the will may be
rectified and nobler purpose be substituted for
inferior desire. Superior motives are addressed
to every understanding. Our Maker has im-
planted detecting conscience, self-respect, and
social affections in every mind elevated above the
physical curtailments of idiotism. The passions
then are the elements of our moral nature; they
cannot be destroyed without our own destruction.

The suspension of their influence is the suspension of consciousness. It is only by the consent of our wills that they are excited into disorder,
and only by our obedience to the laws which our
conscience acknowledges are our passions brought
to act in harmony. They must be placed in their
proper relations to their objects before the perfection of their purpose can be demonstrated: and
as wisely might we say that disease and tempest
frustrate divine wisdom, as impugn the Almighty
because our moral being is liable to disturbance.
Disorder must yet glorify the God that called
light out of darkness. He will vindicate Himself
by teaching the sinful soul in felt weakness to

depend on Omnipotence, and to derive motive, encouragement and means to rise above all merely human affections, by submitting to the beauty and attractiveness of divine example. It needs only the superintendence of a corrected understanding to preserve our passions in order, by keeping them employed in a proper manner. Even in a reformed madhouse we may learn that occupation is the secret of enjoyment; for, however whimsical the delusion, or however impetuous the passion, it may be diverted or innocently gratified by one mind gaining the attention of another. It is by partially yielding to the mistaken interests that absorb the disordered mind that we persuade and acquire the power of conducting it to right associations. It is by a demonstrated concern for the well-being of others that we secure their affections, and it is by contemplating the ways of Providence towards ourselves that we attain holier desires and a full confidence in the hand that helps us.

A little reflection will show us that the effect of one object of emotion can be removed only by the mind being directed to another. Thus anger, the fiercest of our passions, is often arrested by a word, a look, or a thought, reminding us of some tender and beloved association.

The greatest agony which the body can endure is sustained for the sake of those we love. Even the lower animals furnish us with striking examples of the mastery of affection over physical suffering. Addison, in the Spectator, relates a touching instance. A skilful anatomist opened a bitch, and as she lay in the most exquisite tortures, offered her one of her young ones which she immediately began to lick, and for a time seemed insensible of her own pain : on its being removed, she kept her eye fixed on it and commenced a wailing cry, which seemed rather to proceed from the loss of her young than a sense of her own torment. We may well blush to contrast the cruelty of the man with the affection of the dog.

We are all governed by what we love, and are taught rather by what we witness in others than by what we experience in ourselves; by what we see rather than what we know; and the management of our moral feelings is successful according to the demand upon our sympathies. The best moral education is familiarity with generous affections at work, and with the wisdom of law exemplified in society, endeavouring to prevent evil, and proving that God cannot endure that one of his rational creatures should harm another.

By contemplating in others the loveliness of self-government, for unselfish purposes, we find our wishes correspond with theirs, and we love them just in proportion as we understand our true interest and believe in the purity of motive. This is the divine method of teaching—"The life is the light of men."

CHAPTER XII.

THE HIGHEST TRIUMPH OF THE SOUL.

CONCLUSION.

THE triumph of man over pain and difficulty is always achieved by fixing his desire upon the attainment of some prize, and the strength of his determination is proportioned to the value his understanding puts upon the object at which he aims. The highest motive that can inspire the rational will is the approval of God; being associated as it is with the assurance of His perfection and the bestowment of His favour. Hence we find a man, whether savage or civilized, heathen or Christian, ready to endure any suffering rather than forego his reliance upon the being whom he acknowledges as his God. The object of his worship may be false as Juggernaut, or as true as Jehovah, the conscientious votary is still faithful unto death; but vast indeed the difference in the consolation and the reason of the faith; as widely separated as the persuasions of folly and terror from the attractiveness of perfect wisdom and love.

Yet it is most interesting to reflect on the might of man's will in resisting temptation and enduring trial, in obedience to what he believes to be the mandate of the divine mind. This submission of his being to supreme will most wonderfully exhibits man's constitution.   He was made to obey God, and this power depends not on a refined education, for the most untutored exhibit it as heroically, if not so beautifully, as the most informed.   It has been said that it is easier to act the martyr than to conquer one's temper; but these achievements are alike difficult, and require the same lofty conceptions of a higher and holier being, who has a right to demand our self-renunciation from love to His perfections. We may therefore include all sense of duty by which men are governed in the idea of supreme right; and if we find men, as we do, willing to sacrifice themselves, we at once perceive that they possess a power in their own wills to overcome every evil disposition by constant obedience to God, their chief good, and the author of their being.   The mind and body are by Him so proportioned, that one can bear all that can be inflicted on the other, and virtue can stand its ground as long as life; so that a soul well-principled will be sooner separated than subdued.*

The detail given by Catlin of the religious rites

* See Rambler, No. 32.

of the Mandan Indians, although presenting an awful picture of the horrors of ignorance and superstition, yet exhibit also a strong illustration of high moral motive, sustaining and enabling the mind to bear patiently the greatest sufferings of the body. He represents them as voluntarily undergoing the most excruciating agonies, for the purpose of proving their devotedness in the dedication of both body and soul to the Great Spirit.

After a long fast, extensive wounds are inflicted in different parts of their bodies, into which skewers of wood are inserted, by which they are then suspended until the quiverings of the lascerated muscles cease, and all struggle and tremor are over; when, being apparently dead, or as they term it in the keeping of the Great Spirit, they are lowered to the ground, where they are allowed to lie till that Spirit enables them to get up and walk. Other horrid rites of an agonizing kind are added, but this is enough to show that these deluded heroes and voluntary martyrs, with due instruction and example, would have made fine Christians; for they committed their souls to the keeping of the Great Spirit, apparently with as firm a confidence in his power, but alas! without a knowledge of His love, as did Lambert, when consuming in a slow fire by order of the bigoted and cruel Henry, he cried in his torments and in his death, "None but Christ, none but Christ;"

or as did Cranmer, when repenting of the weakness that induced him to subscribe to papal doctrines, he held his hand unflinchingly in the flames until entirely consumed, calling aloud, " This hand has offended, this hand has offended!"

The history of martyrdom supplies a multitude of instances which so convincingly demonstrate the dominion of the soul over the body, as to induce a prevalent belief among those who consider not the might of the human will, that martyrs were generally sustained in their suffering by direct miraculous interference. Nor can we wonder at this notion, for a faith that triumphs over death appears supernatural; belonging not so much to this life as to another, and indeed taking possession of the soul to fix its affections on a nobler world to conduct it thither.

It may be imagined that excessive bodily torment would exhaust the nervous power and terminate in delirium, thus accounting for the raptures expressed on some of those occasions. This may sometimes happen, especially when the infliction is very gradual, and the brain has been previously wearied by feverish anxieties; for our merciful Maker has so ordered our connexion with the body, that when suffering becomes too intense and too continued for the mastery of the will, through the nervous structure, the attention is drawn off from the bodily feeling by mental associations, and from sensible to spiritual impressions, and delightful thoughts then generally take the place of agony. But this delirious ecstacy seems very rarely to have happened with martyrs; for their exalted determination in general maintained a testimony either in prayers or exhortations against demoniac persecution, with clearness and rational freedom till the very moment that death sealed their evidence. That the mind retained its integrity in the midst of flames until the moment of decease, is shown by many facts, as in the instances of Lambert and Cranmer above quoted.

Mr. Hawkes, also being entreated by his friend to give them some token that the fire was not so intolerable but that a man might keep his mind quiet and patient, he assented; and, if so, he promised he would lift his hands above his head before he died. An eye witness states that at the stake he mildly addressed himself to the flames, and when his speech was taken away, and his skin drawn altogether, and his fingers consumed so that all thought him dead, he, in remembrance of his promise, suddenly lifted up his burning hands and clapped them together three times as if in great joy. James Bainham, also having half his arms and legs consumed, spake these words, "Ye look for miracles! Here now ye may see one. This fire is a bed of roses to me."

These witnesses for heaven knew what death is,

but they never felt it. The Lord of life changed torment into delight for them, and converted the fury of flame into a gentle air that wafted their spirits to their kindred; and ere He sent the chariot of salvation He had well assured them that the separation of soul and body is only a symbolic part of death; but that to dwell willingly in the darkness which the smile of perfect love can never dissipate, is death indeed. This struggling after unattainable objects, this fretting because we cannot trust our faithful Creator, this turmoil of selfish passion,—this is death. Reliance upon God for every good, is life. The spirit, elevated and sustained by the divine strength of a Christian's faith, may walk above the turbulence of this world in a path of light, brighter and calmer than that which the moonbeam paves upon the waters, and which terminates only in the pure and serene glory of eternal heaven.

We find then that man, as regards both mind and body, is liable to disease from disturbance originating in the moral nature. His passions are his bane, as well as his blessedness. Now these tendencies to disorder, existing in his constitutional emotions, are to be subdued only by appeals to a power of self-control, to some consenting principle which perceives the reasonableness of obedience to certain laws for the sake of preserving the well-being of one's self in the welfare of others. In short, an appeal to the understanding of the individual for his own benefit, only as a part of a grand system of united individuals.

Conscience proves our personality, and indicates that our nature is not a random result, but that it may be improved or perverted in relation to a future state; for if we have not, nor expect, another state of being, what is the consequence of this life? Why should we regard anything but our own convenience or enjoyment? What then is the value of that word which whispers inwardly—" *Thou* shalt love thy *God* with all thy soul, and thy neighbour as *thyself?*

The arguments of materialists go to establish the notion that health of mind depends on health of body; but the truth seems to be, that what contributes to the one contributes also to the other; for neither can be preserved without obedience to moral as well as physical ordinances. Indeed, it may not be impossible to prove that perfect obedience to moral law would ensure the complete welfare of human nature; and the more we study the operation of our passions on the body, the more we discover of evidence that health of soul is health to the body also; at least we cannot fail to discern that a holy will is the best regulator of desire and of action, and the only warrant of our qualification for an inheritance in light.

The one conclusion of all research on this, as on every other subject, is inevitable. There is certainly some end worthy of man's creation and suited to his spirit, in his advancing struggle after knowledge and goodness, which the economy of earthly existence does not furnish. The purpose of being is not here explained; intelligent desire is not satisfied; the sunshine of truth is only reflected on earth; there is no perfect day to the soul; light direct from its source falls not on the sight; we must imagine the delights of which we are capable but which we cannot here realize; we must live abstractedly if we would live reasonably in holy intimacy with Divine and human science; we must look forward into futurity for the meaning of the past. The present adds but a stone to the grand erection, the design of which is to occupy our contemplation everlastingly; for each individual mind, in its memory and experience, is adding material to material, in an order and for an end at present unknown to itself, but yet manifestly according to the plan of a mind that cannot be disappointed.

The very body, which in health so beautifully obeys us, while the soul seeks only perishing enjoyment, becomes an impediment to our nobler aspirations; and when the spirit awakes to the consciousness of its infinite capacity, its very efforts to be free tend to burst the bonds of the body, which becomes more and more irksome as the mind grows mature; at length the ruinous condition of the earthly tabernacle strengthens the desire for one that is heavenly and eternal; and when the body obeys not, then the attentive believing spirit begins to enjoy true liberty in acquaintance with God's purpose to his creature; and already catching a gleam of glory from beyond the grave, the regenerated man passes through death, and finds it only one step to enter for ever through that gateway into satisfying and endless life.

THE END.

Walton and Mitchell, Printers, 24, Wardour-street.

CPSIA information can be obtained at www.ICGtesting.com
Printed in the USA
LVOW022214091112

306408LV00003B/357/P